BRITAIN'S BIZARRE RAILWAYS

ROBIN JONES

HALSGROVE

385.0941
JON

First published in Great Britain in 2010, reprinted 2012.

Copyright © Robin Jones 2010.

To Vicky and Ross

All rights reserved. No part of this publication may be reproduced,
stored in a retrieval system, or transmitted in any form or by any
means without the prior permission of the copyright holder.

British Library Cataloguing-in-Publication Data
A CIP record for this title is available from the British Library

ISBN 978 0 85704 022 0

HALSGROVE
Halsgrove House,
Ryelands Business Park,
Bagley Road, Wellington, Somerset TA21 9PZ
Tel: 01823 653777   Fax: 01823 216796
email: sales@halsgrove.com

Part of the Halsgrove group of companies
Information on all Halsgrove titles is available at: www.halsgrove.com

Printed and bound in China by Everbest Printing Co Ltd

CONTENTS

Grateful thanks are due to the following
for kindly supplying pictures:

Beamish Museum: 5, 6 lower left, 7 top right; Bodmin
& Wenford Railway: 33, 34 (2); David Buck: 134;
Cambridgeshire County Council: 75; Corsham Heritage
Centre: 103 (right); Maurice Dart collection: 46 (top);
Clive Fairchild: 140, 142: Ffestiniog Railway, Roger
Dimmick: 12, 13 top right, 15 (2), 22 (2), 23, 24, 41, 56,
71; First Great Western 27 (top right); Flat Holm Project:
78 (2); Friends of Clifton Rocks Railway: 67, 68 (2), 69 (3);
Great Laxey Mines Railway: 60 (2), 61(2), 62 (2), Great
Western Society, Frank Dumbleton: 15 (3); K E Hartley
collection/Rod Redman: 42 (2), 43 (2); Taylor Herring: 137;
Hornby: 138 (2), 139 (2), 141; M Hesketh-Roberts/English
Heritage: 102 (2), 103 (left), 104 (2); 105; Mervyn
Leah/Leighton Buzzard Railway: 100 (top); Alan Lewis 108;
Listowel & Ballybunion Railway: 50 (top), 51 (bottom); 52
(2); London Transport Museum: 58 (2), 57 (2), 59 (2);
Paul Miller 89; Richard Mountstephen/Wells &
Walsingham Light Railway: 124 (2); Narrow Gauge
Railway Society: 76, 77 (top); National Railway Museum:
8, 14 bottom, 53 (bottom), 55 (top): Railword: 113 (top);
RobSue888 –Flickr.com: 46; Seaton Tramway: 115 (2), 116;
E R Shepherd: 48 (2); Peter Skuce: 108; South West Trains:
107 (right); David Staines: 32 (bottom); Statfold Barn
Railway and Henry Noon: frontispiece, 72, 74 (main
picture); C H Stocker www.cornish-stocker.com: 64
(main picture); John Stretton: 131; Mauritz Vink/Creative
Commons: 88; Vale of Rheidol Railway:
128; Volks Electric Railway Association: 30, 31 (2);
Nicholas Watts collection: 93 (top);
Mark Wilson: 63 (bottom)

CHAPTER ONE
A MAMMOTH ACHIEVEMENT

NEITHER TREVITHICK, George Stephenson and his son Robert nor anyone else set down hard and fast rules as to what a steam locomotive should look like. The technology was in their day in its infancy and in the race to develop the concept, it was unavoidable that it should have manifested itself in weird and wonderful forms, the like of which soon became obsolete and were never seen again.

Steam engines were developed by necessity, because of a shortage of horses, and became known as the iron horse. But why stop there: could there be a steam donkey, a steam mule, or maybe…a steam elephant.

In the latter case, there certainly could be. And in one of the most testing feats of modern-day heritage engineering, hampered by the total lack of original plans, Beamish Museum in County Durham managed to bring one of these mammoths back from extinction.

In 1812 the Middleton Railway became the first commercial railway to successfully use steam locomotives. Colliery manager John Blenkinsop asked Matthew Murray of Fenton, Murray and Wood in Holbeck, Leeds, to produce one, and he designed a locomotive based on Trevithick's *Catch-Me-Who-Can* called *Salamanca*. William Hedley and Timothy Hackworth's *Puffing Billy* from 1813 survives at the Science Museum, while Beamish created a working replica of it in 2005. Another engineer in the north-east, the cradle of the steam railways, was William Chapman, who had a rope works at Willington. He built chain-drive locomotives in 1813, and the following year, George Stephenson completed his first steam engine, 16 years before *Rocket*.

An account book from Chapman's works now owned by Beamish lists a payment on 20 June 1815 for 'six waggon wheels for locomotive' and a kit of locomotive parts.

Apparently this forgotten locomotive underwent trials at Washington, while an oil painting – the earliest known one of a steam locomotive – showed it hauling chaldron wagons at Wallsend.

Constructed by Hawks and Company of Gateshead, a long-defunct firm of locomotive builders, it was a Steam Elephant: like the mammoths of old, its existence was consigned to the mists of time and left for researchers to rediscover.

The modern-day Steam Elephant stands outside Beamish Museum's replica 1825 engine shed, which houses locomotives on its Pockerley Waggonway.

The oil painting of 1820 is the best out of a handful of artefacts to show that a Steam Elephant ever existed. It shows the original Steam Elephant, or one of them, hauling a load of chaldron wagons towards the docks at Wallsend.

The Steam Elephant, the first standard gauge steam locomotive to be built in the 21st century, heads a train on the Pockerley Waggonway, which accurately reflects the time when the virgin Durham countryside began to be carved up by steam-powered mineral railways.

The replica Steam Elephant stands next to Beamish Museum's working replica of Locomotion No 1, the engine built for the world's first public steam railway, the Stockton & Darlington, which opened in 1825.

It was designed by Chapman for mining engineer John Buddle, nicknamed 'King of the Coal Trade' in the north east, who became manager at Wallsend Colliery in 1806 and introduced the safety lamp invented by Humphry Davy there.

The Steam Elephant was a six-wheeled locomotive with a centre-flue boiler having two vertical cylinders set into its top centreline. The cylinders drove slidebar-mounted beams which turned crankshafts driving the axles through reduction gears between the frames.

Running on a line believed to approximate to standard gauge, its distinctive feature was a tall, tapering chimney, It weighed about 7.5 tons and had a top speed of around 4.5mph.

The water for the boiler was pre-heated before it was pumped into the boiler in a jacket placed around the bottom of the chimney. This method not only saved fuel but also stopped the problems caused by pumping cold water straight into a hot boiler.

At first unsuccessful because its weight broke the wooden rails at the colliery, as soon as they were replaced by metal ones, it became a veritable workhorse, or rather 'workelephant', and operated at Wallsend until least the mid-1820s. It may have been rebuilt for County Durham's Hetton collieries and worked there for further decade. It has also been suggested that it was so successful that more than one Steam Elephant worked at Wallsend...the world's first trunk railway, dare we ask?

Once the researchers at Beamish had established the identity of the mystery locomotive, it was decided to use just the oil painting and four other contemporary pictures, combined with knowledge of other early locomotives, to draw up a blueprint for a modern-day replica – which was built over six years at a cost of £360,000.

The project was headed by Jim Rees, keeper of industry at the museum and locomotive driver on its Pockerley Waggonway early railways demonstration line, and Andy Guy, a library researcher.

The final assembly was completed by locomotive builder Alan Keef at his workshops in Ross-on-Wye, and the new Elephant was launched in 2002 to widespread acclaim. While the new Elephant is built to standard gauge, few heritage railways today could run it, because of the problem of bridges and the jumbo-sized chimney.

Looking back, its design seems to have led to a technological cul-de-sac. It did a job on a local basis, but was too cumbersome to compete with other early locomotives to take the concept much further forward.

Chapman also invented the bogie, while it was Buddle who first installed metal springs on engines: and both innovations shaped the course of steam locomotive development, long outliving their locomotive that time nearly forgot.

Nonetheless, the 21st-century Steam Elephant offers an invaluable window into those embryonic times.

The Steam Elephant with Beamish Museum's replica of Puffing Billy, *which was completed in 2005.*

A contemporary engraving shows India's first steam locomotive being delivered – hauled by elephants!

CHAPTER TWO

THE ULTIMATE GREEN LINE

WE OFTEN HEAR would-be politicians talk at length about green transport and a switch to rail, only for them to go mysteriously silent on the issue as soon as they are elected and the costs involved are explained.

Yet in Britain we have an example of a perfect eco-friendly line.

First, it produced no smoke or exhaust fumes – as the sole traction was horse power, powered by locally-grown hay and oats – in other words, pure renewable energy.

Secondly, there was no heavy industry involved in the manufacture of its 'rails', for they were granite blocks hewn out of local quarries. As such they required little if any maintenance, and unlike conventional rails, would never rust away.

Not only that, but the railway was all but indestructible and would require a huge and very uneconomic effort to lift it. That is why much of it is still there today, on the eastern edge of Dartmoor, and it is free to be walked by anyone.

The uppermost part of the Haytor Tramway is still visible and easily walkable. Haytor is on the horizon to the left.

A contemporary print of the Haytor quarries in their heyday of the 1820s, showing granite blocks being moved on branches of the tramway.

Prized for its fine grain and high quality, Dartmoor granite has been a source of building material from neolithic times when it was used to build the stone rows and circles which survive on the barren uplands.

Ball clay, which is formed by decomposing granite, was mined in the Bovey Tracey area from the 1730s for use in pottery, and was taken by pack mules for shipping from Newton Abbot via the estuary of the River Teign.

James Templer, who inherited the 80,000-acre Stover Estate near Newton Abbot in 1792, that year opened the 1¾-mile Stover Canal from Ventiford near the estate to Newton Abbot to make the export of ball clay and locally-mined lignite and iron ore easier. Using the canal, ball clay was supplied to the Wedgwood potteries at Stoke-on-Trent.

His son George developed the family's granite quarries at Haytor on a commercial basis in response to demand for quality building materials, and realised that he would never make a fortune by using horse-drawn carts taking heavy granite blocks slowly over moorland.

He decided to build a railway, but among those still to be convinced of the merits of steam traction which was still very much in its infancy, he opted to play it safe and go for a horse-drawn tramway.

The 4ft 3in gauge track was made from irregular granite blocks quarried at Haytor and cut to size, with a rebate carved in each for carrying the iron wheels of the wagons.

The guiding flanges that kept the wagons on the rails were part of the rails, a system known as a plateway or flanged way. It had, and still has, all the recognised features of 'normal'

Above left: A curving section of the tramway on the approach to Haytor.

Above centre: A point leads to a siding above Haytor Vale.

Above right: Lilies float on a pool in one of the Haytor quarries.

The only surviving bridge on the tramway crosses the Bovey Leat near Chapple Farm, about two miles west of Bovey Tracey.

A granite 'point' frog.

railway trackwork, like points, crossovers and sidings. At the points, the wheels were guided by wooden 'point tongues' made from oak, pivoted on the granite-block rails. In many ways, it resembled a child's Brio train set, where the track sections are carved from wood.

A network of six branch lines and sidings resembling a later railway marshalling yard served the booming Haytor quarries, and a the 8½-mile tramway descended from the 1300ft-high summit along a circuitous route into the Bovey valley, reaching Ventiford basin at the northern end of the Stover Canal, which had been extended westwards to meet it in 1820. From there, the granite was carried by canal boat to the New Quay at Teignmouth for export by ship.

Going uphill, the empty wagons were hauled back to the quarries by teams of horses, but downwards, the loaded wagons moved by gravity to Ventiford.

The Haytor Tramway, as it came to be known, was all but unique, the only other known example of this type of railway being a very short 3ft gauge limestone line at Conisborough near Doncaster.

The wooden flat-topped wagons had iron flangeless wheels and ran in trains of 12 drawn by around 18 horses, walking single file in front for the upward journey and at the rear for the downward trips. The only braking facility was provided by the horses and long wooden poles forced against the wheels.

The tramway was officially opened on 16 September 1820 that year amidst public celebrations on Haytor Down, where George Templer held a massive fete. Thomas Taverner, an old sailor, wrote a poem about it:

Nineteen stout horses it was known,
From Holwell Quarry drew the stone,
And mounted on twelve-wheeled car
'Twas safely brought from Holwell Tor

The '12-wheeled car' refers to 12 wagons with wheels.

During the 1820s, thousands of tons of granite shipped via the tramway each year.

In 1825, it carried granite for the building of London Bridge, the same one which in the 1960s was sold to the Americans. Part of the British Museum, the old General Post Office in London and the Waltham Monument in Ludgate Circus were built from Haytor granite in the 19th century.

George Templer died in a hunting accident in 1843, and after many years of competition from cheaper Cornish granite, the Haytor Quarries had all but closed by 1858, with the tramway long since fallen into disuse.

When the Moretonhampstead & South Devon Railway Company built a 12¼-mile line linking the Dartmoor town to Isambard Kingdom Brunel's South Devon Railway in the 1860s, the easternmost mile of the tramway was used for part of it.

The tramway's owner, the Duke of Somerset, insisted that new interchange sidings between the old and new lines were created a mile south of Bovey Tracey, complete with a crane for lifting blocks of granite, despite the fact it had been disused for many years.

Around 1905 a scheme to electrify the remaining part of the old tramway and run a passenger-carrying tram service was launched, and reached the stage where a small power station was built for it, but the scheme fizzled out. The power station was used by Bovey's clay potteries until it fell into ruin.

The Moretonhampstead branch passed into Great Western and then British Railways ownership, but lost its passenger services on 28 February 1959, four years before Beeching wielded his axe. Attempts to preserve it failed as part of it was retained for goods, in particular ball clay traffic, and it was eventually cut back to Heathfield. In 2011, the overgrown line was refurbished for a new Colas Rail Freight timber traffic contract from chipboard manufacturer Kronospan, while the nearby Stover Canal is the subject of a restoration bid.

The tramway itself is now a Scheduled Ancient Monument and in recent times efforts have been made to maintain it as such. It can be seen at several points and walked for long distances, while the Haytor quarries have been designated as a Site of Special Scientific Interest, and are one of the most visited and beautiful parts of Dartmoor National Park.

Teignmouth's New Quay in 1827 with a large crane and blocks of cut granite brought in by canal barge ready to be loaded on to ships.

A final destination for the Haytor granite: London Bridge in 1900.

CHAPTER THREE
WHAT GOES UP...

SOMETIME BEFORE 1687, a scientist called Isaac Newton was sitting in the garden of his home at Woolsthorpe Manor in Lincolnshire when an apple fell on his head.

It was that year that his *Philosophiæ Naturalis Principia Mathematica*, in which he changed the course of science with his landmark theories on gravity, was published. The apple tree is still there.

Between 1833 and 1836, the Festiniog Railway was built for carrying slate from the quarries around Blaenau Ffestiniog to Porthmadog, where it was loaded on to waiting ships in the harbour.

Although steam traction by then had begun taking off in a big way elsewhere, the Festiniog was designed to be operated by horse traction one way – and gravity the other, in true Newtonian style!

The wagons were hauled up the 13½ miles from the harbour to the quarries, loaded and sent to roll back down again, along the more or less continuous 1-in-80 gradient. The horses followed in 'dandy' wagons.

To make gravity traction work, the line followed natural contours, with cuttings and embankments built of stone and slate blocks without mortar to cross valleys and streams where necessary. Before the Moelwyn Tunnel was completed in 1844, the slate trains had to be worked

A gravity slate train running during the Ffestiniog Railway's Quirks & Curiosities gala which was held over the May Day weekend in 2010.

over Moelwyn mountain by an incline, which interrupted the passage of the gravity trains.

The fastest journey time from Quarry Terminus in Blaenau to Boston Lodge was one hour 32 minutes, including three stops. From Boston Lodge, the slate wagons were hauled over The Cob, the giant stone causeway built across the Traeth Mawr estuary, to harbour by horses. The empty wagon trains from Boston Lodge to Quarry Terminus, took nearly six hours, each train comprising four sections, each hauled by a horse and made up of eight empty slate wagons and a dandy wagon.

Health and safety officials pause for breath here: the gravity trains each had a pair of brakesmen travelling on them, controlling the speed by applying brakes as required. It is said that some tourist passengers were conveyed, without official sanction, as early as 1850.

Steam locomotives in the form of George England 0-4-0 saddle tanks were introduced in October 1863 in order to facilitate the running of longer slate trains. Two years later, the line became Britain's first narrow-gauge railway to officially carry passengers.

A Festiniog Railway gravity slate train passes Ddualt in the 1920s.

The downhill trains continued to run entirely by gravity, but uphill journeys were much faster, despite the longer trains. Timings were cut to one hour 50 minutes in each direction, the trains passing at the midway point of Tan-y-Bwlch.

The slate trains could be more than 80 wagons long, and in such cases, three rather than two brakesmen were needed. Around one wagon in every six had a brake,

At first, the down trains were run in four separate but uncoupled sections, comprising loaded slate wagons, goods wagons, passenger carriages and the locomotive running light behind. This arrangement lasted only briefly, and the passenger and goods sections were soon combined into a single train pulled by the locomotive.

Loaded gravity slate trains continued to run until the end of passenger services in 1939.

Slate trains were from then onwards operated three days each week, but were all locomotive hauled. Slate traffic over the line, which had been declining since the 1920s, finally ended on 1 August 1946, and thereafter the Festiniog Railway went to sleep as Mother Nature began to reclaim it, until the revivalists stepped in.

Gravity trains were by no means unique to the Festiniog: as we saw earlier, the Haytor Tramway also followed contours on its way from quarry to harbour, and similar operations were undertaken there.

Porthmadog harbour in the days of sail, where slate from the Blaenau quarries was taken for export.

However, there is nowhere else in Britain today where you have the occasional chance to see a gravity train in action. The revived Ffestiniog Railway runs them on special occasions, when it is possible to travel in restored slate wagons, at very low speed, under the utmost of supervision over part of the line.

It is indeed strange that a railway famous for its magnificent fleet of Victorian steam engines including the double Fairlies should still be able to run trains without using any form of traction at all!

CHAPTER FOUR
VICTORY OF THE NARROW MINDED

Replica broad gauge 2-2-2 Fire Fly, *representing state-of-the-art steam traction of the 1840s, inside the Burlescombe transhipment shed at Didcot Railway Centre.*

ON 2 MARCH 2005, the first all-new express passenger steam locomotive to be built in Britain for 51 years was proudly launched into traffic.

Built to a design that was once capable of breaking world speed records, it will never appear on the country's national network. Instead, it must by needs spending its working life running up and down a few hundred yards of track.

The engine is called *Fire Fly*, and it is a full-size replica of the first of the Firefly class of 2-2-2s built to a design by Great Western Railway locomotive superintendent Daniel Gooch.

Its appearance gives away its ancestry: it is as if it has been transported from through time from the 1840s when massive gleaming brass steam domes, stovepipe chimneys, boiler cladding made from wooded planks, massive single driving wheels and minimalist cabs were cutting edge technology. To a modern viewer, it looks both absurd and magnificent.

You can ride behind *Fire Fly* on the demonstration line at Didcot Railway Centre, where

This watercolour by Sean Bolan in the possession of the National Railway Museum at York shows a member of Daniel Gooch's Iron Duke class at Chippenham c 1850.

two replica period carriages, one open and the other enclosed, have been built to accompany the locomotive. Yet for any other revenue-earning passenger-carrying purpose, it is totally useless – because since 1892, there have been no routes on which it could physically operate.

The Fireflys were, of course, classic broad gauge locomotives, built to 7ft 0¼in gauge, at a time when most of the emerging British railway network was rapidly conforming to George Stephenson's 4ft 8½in gauge, which eventually won the day.

The GWR broad gauge was the brainchild of its engineer Isambard Kingdom Brunel, who was given the task of supervising the building of a railway from London to Bristol in 1835, at the age of 27.

Brunel and his father Marc were engineers who allowed science and logic rather than popular expert opinion to shape their thinking: it was said that a tunnel could not be successfully bored beneath the Thames in London, but the pair achieved it. When asked to survey the route of the GWR, young Isambard refused to produce the cheapest line, insisting only the best was good enough, and won the day.

Back in 1835, there was no national rail network as such, and engineers were left to very much do their own thing. There was no legal obligation on railways to adopt a particular gauge. Indeed, until the development of the steam locomotive, nobody had ever specified exactly how far apart the rails must be on a railway.

Until the 19th century, railways were, as we have seen, horse-drawn local affairs serving mines, collieries, quarries or factories, and the track gauge was chosen that suited the wagons that would be carried. Such measurements were based on horse-drawn carts, which had to be of a sensible size for the horse to pull. The distance between the cartwheels would therefore be typically in the range of 4ft-5ft.

George Stephenson measured the average distance between the wheels of the carts that ran on the colliery lines of the North East where he worked as an engineman, and came up with 4ft 8½in: a reasonable choice, being not too narrow and not too wide. As history records, a chain of often-chance circumstances led to this particular gauge becoming standard not only throughout Britain but also North America, most of western Europe and much of the rest of the world.

However, prior to his appointment to the GWR, Isambard had visited both the world's first public steam railway, the Stockton & Darlington, and the first inter-city line, the Liverpool & Manchester, and was not wholly impressed by either.

When it came to his turn to build a railway, he took a blank sheet of paper, and came up with 7ft 0¼in gauge (the purpose of the quarter inch being to accommodate clearances). He justified his highly-controversial choice on scientific grounds, and it remains the widest gauge to have been used for an extensive public passenger system.

Brunel argued successfully that 7ft 0¼in gave clear advantages in reducing the centre of

On 4 April 2010, Fire Fly hauls its recently-completed second-class coach and third-class open coach along the Didcot demonstration line.

Top: *The interior of the new broad gauge second-class carriage at Didcot.*

Above: *GWR third-class travel 1840s style!*

Above left: North Star, *the GWR's first locomotive, reassembled following its destruction by William Stanier at Swindon in 1906 and now displayed in the town's STEAM museum.*

Above right: *The National Railway Museum's replica of* Iron Duke, *in the Great Hall at York.*

A contemporary sketch of Isambard Kingdom Brunel.

gravity of rolling stock by mounting coach and wagon bodies between the wheels rather than above them. Also, the wider gauge would accommodate much larger and more powerful locomotives and carriages and wagons with a greater capacity.

Yet he conceded from the start that it would be impossible for GWR trains to run over other lines built to 4ft 8½in gauge. This was the single flaw that would within 60 years see his broad gauge all but wiped off the face of the earth.

Twenty years earlier, Marc Brunel had installed a sawmill at Chatham Dockyard with rails 7ft apart, It may well have been the gauge of this obscure railway that influenced his son.

Ironically, it was Robert Stephenson, son of 4ft 8½in gauge promoter George, who built Brunel's first locomotive at his Newcastle-upon-Tyne works. The 2-2-2 *North Star* had been constructed for the 5ft 6in gauge New Orleans Railway but regauged to 7ft 0¼in, and it hauled the first GWR passenger train over the initial section of 24 miles from Paddington to Maidenhead on 4 June 1838.

In June 1841, the GWR finally linked Paddington to Bristol Temple Meads, with Brunel taking available technology and resources to the limits with landmark features such as Sonning Cutting, the elliptical-arched bridge at Maidenhead and the magnificent Box Tunnel.

His own locomotive designs were of questionable quality. However, he pulled off another masterstroke with his appointment of 21-year-old Daniel Gooch as locomotive superintendent. Gooch designing a more powerful and larger version of the Star class, the Fireflys. The first, named *Fire Fly*, was delivered by Jones, Turner & Evans of Newton-le-Willows on 12 March 1840.

Fire Fly hauled the directors' special to mark the opening of the line beyond Twyford to

Reading. The outward run from Paddington took just 45 minutes for the 36 miles, whilst on the return an astonishing 58mph was reached and the 31 miles from Twyford to the capital completed in just 37 minutes. For the early Victorians, this was space-age technology.

Brunel and Gooch established Swindon Works where the GWR began building their own locomotives, including the similarly-groundbreaking Iron Duke class. Indeed, the GWR broad gauge Paddington-Didcot trains in 1848 were not bettered for speed until the Class 125 High Speed Trains appeared in the 1970s.

After completing the GWR, Brunel engineered the Bristol & Exeter Railway, also built to broad gauge. Driven by Gooch, Fire Fly class locomotive *Actaeon* covered the 194 miles from Paddington in five hours on 1 May 1844. The return journey was even better, taking just four hours 40 minutes, a world-record average of 40.1mph over both legs. Also, on Somerset's Wellington bank a Bristol & Exeter Railway broad gauge 4-2-4 tank engine was recorded at 81.8mph.

In isolation therefore, there was much to commend Brunel's bizarre choice of gauge. Yet despite its headline-demanding feats, by then it was out of sync with the rest of Britain.

Parliament recommended banning broad gauge as early as 1845 in the interests of 'one size fits all' uniformity and to eradicate the nuisance of passengers having to change trains and freight being unloaded and loaded again, even though it was conceded that 7ft 0¼in was superior in terms of speed and safety. By then there were 274 miles of broad gauge track but 1901 miles of 4ft 8½in gauge lines: something of a marketing triumph for the Stephenson gauge!

Brunel remained defiant in his belief that his system was the best, but nonetheless in 1847 the GWR by needs must began laying mixed gauge, between Gloucester and Cheltenham, in order to accommodate through trains from other companies. The GWR built its first standard gauge engines in 1855, a year after absorbing its first 4ft 8½in gauge lines, the Shrewsbury & Chester and Shrewsbury & Birmingham railways.

The Brunel broad gauge empire eventually stretched north to Wolverhampton, south to Weymouth and westwards to Penzance and Milford Haven, by 1866 extending to 1427 miles, including 387 miles of mixed gauge.

Isambard Brunel died in 1859, and within a decade, the great railway he had created realised the writing was on the wall for broad gauge, and began converting major routes to 4ft 8½in. Despite this U-turn, some new lines were still built to 7ft 0¼in gauge, the last being the short St Ives branch which opened on 1 June 1877, although there was a short extension to the freight-only Sutton Harbour branch in Plymouth in 1879. The final GWR broad gauge engine to emerge from Swindon Works was Rover class 4-2-2 No 24 *Tornado* in July 1888.

Three years later, the GWR board finally agreed to wash its hands of broad gauge altogether.

The Engine House at Swindon Works in the 1840s, as sketched by JC Bourne.

The smallest broad gauge engine ever built, Tiny *is displayed inside the South Devon Railway's Buckfastleigh museum.*

The last broad gauge 'Cornishman' express leaves Paddington station for Penzance at 10.15am on Friday 20 May 1892. The last broad gauge train out of Paddington was the 5pm Plymouth train.

The final broad gauge passenger train left Penzance for Swindon at 9.57pm on 20 May 1892, witnessed by large crowds who delayed its departure. The train stopped at every station between Penzance and Exeter, with each stationmaster having to confirm to the inspector on board that all broad gauge stock had been removed from his station.

During the following weekend of 21/22 May, an army of 4200 permanent way workers set about converting the remaining broad gauge lines, which totalled around 171 miles.

Rendered obsolete with nowhere to run, 196 locomotives, 347 carriages and 3544 wagons stood on 15 miles of specially-laid sidings at Swindon waiting to be scrapped. They were shunted into the works' cutting shop by the last Brunel broad gauge engines to run, South Devon Railway 4-4-0 saddle tanks *Leopard* and *Stag*, used until June 1893 until they too met the same fate.

Just two were preserved by the GWR, *North Star* and *Lord Of The Isles*. Astonishingly, they were cut up at Swindon Works in 1906 to create storage space under the orders of one William Stanier, who said he was concerned not with the past but the future, and three decades later achieved immortal fame as the designer of the great Pacific locomotives for the London, Midland & Scottish Railway.

His boss at Swindon, George Jackson Churchward, who had been on holiday at the time, was horrified at this action. He salvaged sufficient parts of *North Star* for it to be reassembled as a stationary exhibit in 1925, and it is now displayed in STEAM - Museum of the Great Western Railway, at Swindon.

The sole surviving original main line company Brunel broad gauge locomotive is the South Devon Railway's 0-4-0 vertical-boilered tank engine No 151 *Tiny*, which was also the smallest. Bought to replace horses on Plymouth's Sutton Harbour branch, it was withdrawn in 1883 and sent for use as a stationary boiler at Newton Abbot works. There it was restored and exhibited on one of Newton Abbot station's platform from 1927, and is today a key exhibit in the modern-day South Devon Railway's Buckfastleigh station museum. Gauge apart, it bears no resemblance whatsoever to the steam behemoths that made the GWR the best railway in the world in Brunel's day.

The operational railway heritage movement, which began with the volunteer takeover of the closure-threatened Talyllyn Railway in 1951, has achieved many miracles since then, not least of all the construction of replica locomotives to voids left by the extinction of key classes.

The National Railway Museum at York had a replica Iron Duke class 4-2-2 built for the Great Western 150 celebrations in 1985, using parts from two standard gauge industrial Austerity 0-6-0 saddle tanks including a boiler, and a short running line was laid outside. It became the first broad gauge engine to steam in Britain since 1893.

The Fire Fly project began with the rediscovery at Paddington of Gooch's original drawings for the class, and in 1982 retired Royal Navy Commander John Mosse founded the Firefly Trust to build a replica. Building began in 1987, and the project eventually moved to the Great Western Society's Didcot base, where it ran under its own power for the first time on 2 March 2005. It was the first brand new main line express passenger steam locomotive built for use in Britain since unique BR Standard 8P Pacific No 71000 *Duke of Gloucester* in 1954, and the first main line steam locomotive to appear since BR Standard 9F 2-10-0 *Evening Star* in 1960.

Elsewhere, the Dalzell Iron & Steel Works in Motherwell went one better than Brunel in buying three 10ft 11in gauge Barclay 0-4-0 saddle tanks to haul ladles of molten slag.

There is one location in Britain, heritage venues apart, where 7ft 0¼in gauge is still in commercial use. An electric crane runs along a 151ft-long track at the National Rivers Authority depot in Reading. Stopping a few inches short, the cable-operated Cairngorm Mountain Railway which opened in 2001 is built to 6ft 6¾in gauge.

Yet again, there is one reason why, despite its advantages, the world might be better off without broad gauge. A guy bearing a loose resemblance to Charlie Chaplin once drew up his own plans for a 9ft 9ins gauge mega-railway network spanning Europe, one which would be capable of carrying untold amounts of military hardware and even ships behind monstrous locomotives. Thanks to events in the spring of 1945, he never had the opportunity to turn his dream into reality. His name was Adolf Hitler.

Meanwhile, Brunel may have lost one argument, but in 2010, his GWR main line from London to Bristol was shortlisted for a bid for UNESCO World Heritage status because of its resounding historical importance. Maybe it was not so bizarre after all.

Rows upon rows of perfectly serviceable broad gauge locomotives await the cutter's torch at Swindon in 1892.

The GWR coat of arms.

CHAPTER FIVE
TWO HEADS ARE BETTER THAN ONE

Little Wonder, the first Festiniog Railway double Fairlie which made its builder a fortune, at Porthmadog in the 1870s, hauling a mixed train of slate wagons and passenger coaches.

THE INVENTION OF the railway locomotive opened up never-before dimensions in transport, and changed the face of global society forever. However, there were situations where the horse and cart (and later the motor car) had a distinct advantage over the steam locomotive.

We could talk about the limited field of vision from traditional main line steam locomotives, where the boiler and chimney blocks the full frontal view, and the driver has to rely on signals and signposts at the lineside. A second drawback, one which concerns us here, is that a steam locomotive, with rare exceptions (such as rack railways or banking engines), is designed to pull a train, rather than push it.

As it is limited to moving on track, it has to turn round when the terminus is reached. Ideally that means the expensive and space-consuming option of installing a turntable, or more commonly on branch lines, the provision of run-round loops, where the locomotive runs past its train and backs on to it at the rear ahead, making the return trip bunker or tender first.

One Victorian engineer, Robert Francis Fairlie, came up with a simple answer to the latter problem: join two engines back to back, and you never have to turn the locomotive!

In the 1840s, Newcastle-upon-Tyne engineer George England founded his own locomotive building company in New Cross, Surrey, and supplied engines to several railways, ranging from the Great Western and Caledonian down to the 1ft 11½in gauge Festiniog Railway in North Wales, which converted to steam haulage in 1863.

England's long-time business associate was Robert Fairlie, who was born in either 1830 or 1831 and trained in the works at both Crewe and Swindon before becoming the Londonderry & Coleraine Railway's locomotive superintendent in 1852. Four years later he joined the Bombay, Baroda & Central India Railway setting himself up as a railway engineering consultant in London in 1859.

Robert Fairlie, the man with double vision.

In April 1862, England brought a criminal action against Fairlie in a case which modern observers might well consider bizarre, and therefore worthy of a brief mention in this book.

England alleged that Fairlie, who had eloped with his daughter Eliza Anne England, in order to obtain a marriage licence, had sworn a false affidavit that her father had consented to the union, which he certainly had not done. After their wedding, the pair ran away to Spain.

However, England was forced to admit that he himself had run away with his present companion, Eliza's mother, even though he had a wife living at that time. He had lived with this lady for several years but could not marry her until his wife died.

Under contemporary English law, a child born out of wedlock was considered nobody's child. Therefore in law she was nothing to do with England and could marry anyone without needing his permission, the Central Criminal Court ruled. Not guilty!

Yet this rift healed sufficiently for England to build the first of a remarkable series of engines for the Festiniog Railway to a Fairlie patent of 1864.

Fairlie believed locomotive design was seriously flawed because weight was wasted on unpowered wheels, including tenders, and they were not intended to be driven in reverse for long periods.

To eliminate turntables, Fairlie's answer was to have a double-ended locomotive, one which carried all its fuel and water aboard the locomotive rather than having a tender and with every axle driven to produce the maximum tractive effort.

His design featured two boilers on the locomotive, joined back-to-back at the firebox ends, with the smokeboxes at each end, and controls at both ends of the central cab to allow the locomotive to be driven equally well in either direction.

The locomotive was supported on two swivelling powered bogies with all wheels driven. Steam was delivered from the boilers to the cylinders via flexible tubing. There were side tanks beside each boiler for the water supply, and bunkers for the fuel located above them.

Fairlie's first double-ended locomotive, *Pioneer*, was built by James Cross & Co of St Helens supplied to the standard gauge Neath & Brecon Railway in 1865, but it was not successful.

However, it was *Little Wonder*, built by England in 1869 for the 1ft 11½in gauge Festiniog, which brought Fairlie fame and fortune.

On 11 February 1870, Fairlie hosted locomotive engineers as far afield as Russia, Mexico, Turkey and Sweden at the Festiniog where he demonstrated *Little Wonder*.

The net result: an order book bursting at the seams, and by 1876, 43 different railways had operated his engines.

However, the only lines where the type was truly successful in the long term were in Mexico, New Zealand and the Festiniog. More than 50 double Fairlies were supplied to Mexico over 40 years, including a fleet of 49 giant 0-6-0+0-6-0s which remained in use until

David Lloyd George, *which in 1982 became the newest of the double Fairlies, heads through slate country with a special to mark the 175th anniversary of the Ffestiniog Railway in 2007.*

Two locomotives, each of which can be driven in either direction. While main line diesels have cabs at the front and rear, double Fairlie Earl of Merioneth *also operates in both directions without having to be turned. It is pictured at the Blaenau Ffestiniog interchange station alongside Western Region diesel hydraulic D1015* Western Champion *heading Pathfinder Tours 'Western Slater' charter from Didcot.*

The oldest surviving Ffestiniog double Fairlie, Livingston Thompson.

the 1920s.

Many owners reported dissatisfaction with the limited capacity for fuel and water, the flexible steam pipes being prone to leakage and wasting of power and the absence of unpowered wheels, which on traditional steam engines act as stabilisers.

For those not adventurous enough to buy a double-ended locomotive, Fairlie produced 'single' versions, with were effectively a double Fairlie cut in half. These proved popular in the USA.

Fairlie gave the Festiniog Railway Company a perpetual license to use the Fairlie locomotive patent without restriction in return for using the line to demonstrate *Little Wonder* – which became the first of six to be owned by the company.

George England died in 1878 and Fairlie followed on 31 July 1885. *Little Wonder* was worn out by 1882 and was scrapped.

The Festiniog's second double Fairlie to arrive was *James Spooner*, which became the line's No 8. Built under licence by Avonside, it ran until 1933 when it too was scrapped.

A third double Fairlie, No 10 *Merddin Emrys*, named after the sixth-century Welsh poet,

Merddin Emrys *at Porthmadog Harbour station in 1935.*

was delivered in 1879 and is still in service today. It underwent a major rebuild in 1987/8 with new tanks.

No 11 *Livingston Thompson* was built at the line's own Boston Lodge Works in 1886. Now out of service, it is on static display in the Great Hall at the National Railway Museum in York.

The Festiniog Railway fell derelict after World War Two, but following the success of the volunteer-led Talyllyn Railway revival in 1951, the line was similarly taken over by enthusiasts in 1954, under the leadership of businessman Alan Pegler, who later, in 1963, bought *Flying Scotsman* from British Railways. The revivalists reopened the railway in stages easgtwards from Porthmadog Harbour station and after performing the biggest volunteer-led

Merddin Emrys hauling the Ffestinog Railway's vintage train, with two 'bug box' quarrymen's coaches immediately behind the engine, along Tank Curve.

civil engineering feat in Europe by constructing a spiral loop and deviation around Llyn Ystradau, a hydro-electric power scheme reservoir which flooded part of the line, the heritage era finally reached Blaenau Ffestiniog on 25 May 1982.

More motive power was needed as the restored line grew longer, and the revivalists decided to continue the Boston Lodge tradition by building their own locomotive. So a new double Fairlie 0-4-4-0 *Earl of Meirioneth* with modern box-like side tanks, emerged from the works in 1979.

It was so well received that a second, *David Lloyd George*, which has a more conventional rounded appearance, emerged three years later.

The original Festiniog (the modern-day company has changed its name to 'Ffestiniog', replacing the 'f' omitted from the original Act of Parliament'), also had a single Fairlie in its fleet, in the form of 1876-built *Taliesin*, which was scrapped in 1935. A replica was built at Boston Lodge in 1999, using a few parts from the original.

In June 2004, the Gwendreath Railway Society discovered that two boilers from scrapped standard gauge double Fairlies had been rediscovered in Burry Port in South Wales. It is believed that one of the boilers belonged to an 0-4-4-0T variously named *Pioneer* and *Mountaineer* which in 1869 was only the second engine to be built by the Fairlie Steam & Carriage Company and which was supplied to the Burry Port & Gwendraeth Valleys Railway. The other boiler is believed to come from 0-6-6-0T *Victoria*, a very early double Fairlie returned by a dissatisfied customer in Queensland and sold to the Burry Port line. Both scrapped around 1900, the boilers survived six feet underground as stormwater culverts.

Elsewhere in the world, double Fairlie *Josephine* is preserved at Dunedin in New Zealand's South Island, and a 60cm gauge double Fairlie tramway engine from a French narrow gauge line is displayed in the Dresden Transport Museum in Germany.

While the sight of double-ended engines never fails to delight visitors to the Ffestiniog, which remains inextricably linked with their design and use, was Fairlie so wide of the mark?

Most types of main line diesel and electric locomotives today have cabs at both ends, eradicating the need for turntables or tuning triangles. The concept of the steam railmotor, a carriage with a steam motor bogie built into one end and a cab into another, evolved into both the steam-hauled auto train and the diesel railcar, both of which can be controlled from either end and need no run-round loops. The next step was the introduction of diesel and electric multiple units, which comprise virtually all main line passenger trains in Britain today.

So was Robert Fairlie really wide of the mark, or years ahead of his time?

Not only did the Ffestiniog Railway revivalists restore the line, but resumed double Fairlie building. Earl of Merioneth *appearing in 1979.*

CHAPTER SIX
BRUNEL'S HOOVERWAY

SOME YEARS AGO I was shown an alternative vacuum cleaner system for the ordinary domestic house.

Instead of having a traditional model which you push around the floor, the cleaner was permanently fixed to one point in the house. It provided suction to a network of pipes fitted within the wall cavities, and there were a series of plug points into which the hose could be clipped. So all you had to do to clean the floors was to carry a lightweight hose around, not push the cleaner itself.

What if someone was to turn the steam locomotive concept inside out in the same way? That is exactly what happened when Isambard Kingdom Brunel began looking for the next leap forward in transport technology.

Instead of having dirty smoky locomotives showering cinders over crew and passengers alike, why not dispense with the locomotive altogether – and have a stationary steam engine at the side of the track pulling the trains along? Only in Brunel's case, it was not achieved by cable or rope, but by a vacuum pipe placed between the tracks, with the steam engine powering a pump to create the vacuum.

It was brilliant – and it worked. Yet it was too far ahead of Brunel's time, and the available technology.

After completing the Bristol & Exeter Railway, Brunel had Plymouth in his sights and was appointed engineer of the South Devon Railway, which was also to be built to 7ft 0¼in broad gauge. The planned route would cross the foothills of Dartmoor, with steep gradients which would later become legendary in the records of Great Western Railway locomotive feats – Hemerdon, Dainton and Rattery. However, Brunel

The pumping station at Dawlish in a painting by Condy, with the vacuum pipe running between the rails.

A rare surviving section of atmospheric railway vacuum pipe on display at Didcot Railway Centre.

A Dalkey & Kingstown Atmospheric Railway train arriving at Kingstown, as portrayed in The Illustrated London News *on 6 January 1844.*

had doubts that the steam locomotives of the day would be able to effectively tackle them.

In September 1844, Brunel and his locomotive engineer Daniel Gooch witnessed a demonstration by inventors Samuel Clegg, a gas lighting pioneer, and Jacob Samuda, a marine engineering expert, of an 'atmospheric' train on Ireland's 1½-mile-long Dalkey & Kingstown Railway. The pair had patented their new system of propulsion on 3 January 1838.

It comprised a cast-iron tube laid between rails and sealed by airtight valves at each end. A piston linked to the bottom of a carriage was pushed past the valve into the tube, and huge stationary steam engines at intervals along the lineside pumped air out of the tube, generating a vacuum ahead of the piston.

The greater pressure of the atmosphere behind the piston would force it along the tube and pull the carriage with it, eliminating the need for an engine. Indeed, it was basically a giant version of a domestic vacuum cleaner.

Isambard Brunel and his father Marc had been dreaming of producing a better alternative to the steam locomotive for more than a decade, wasting a small fortune on developing their Gaz Engine, intended to be powered by pressurized carbonic gas, and which did not work.

When he saw atmospheric propulsion at work, he believed he had found the future of rail transport, a new system which was clean, silent and fast, with lighter and more efficient trains. Because atmospheric traction did not depend on the adhesion of heavy locomotives to the rails, he could economise on earthworks, cutting costs while allowing steep inclines. To boost power on the gradients, all you had to do would be to increase the diameter of the vacuum pipe, add a second pipe, or build a bigger pumping engine.

Brunel found a fellow supporter in none other than Prime Minister Sir Robert Peel who wanted to see all railways adopt the atmospheric system.

During the Railway Mania of the 1840s, railway share prices soared, and anyone wanting to build a new line easily found financial backing.

After the Dublin & Kingstown Railway came the London & Croydon in 1846, the 1.4-mile Paris & St-Germain Railway from Bois de Vezinet to St-Germain in Paris in 1847... and the South Devon Railway.

The project received its royal assent on 4 July 1844, and Brunel made plans to build the entire 52-mile line as an atmospheric system.

Nine huge Italianate engine houses were built at three-mile intervals along the route from Exeter to Teignmouth, which in itself was a gargantuan feat of engineering, hugging the foot of storm-lashed cliffs and divided from the sea by a wall, a series of tunnels taking it from one sandy cover to another en route.

This initial stretch opened on 30 May 1846 – using steam engines at first, while the vacuum tube and leather and metal valve of the atmospheric system continued to be laid.

Two public atmospheric trains ran over the line from 13 September 1847, and from

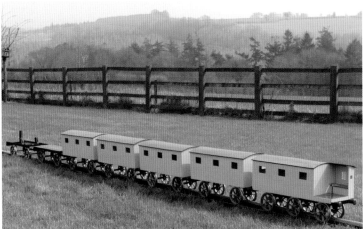

10 January 1848 services were extended to Newton Abbot, with some freight being carried as well as a piston carriage.

The high speeds promised by Brunel were indeed achieved, a very impressive 68mph with a 28-ton load and 35mph with 100 tons. However, the 20 miles from Exeter to Newton Abbot with four stops took a slow 55 minutes because one train had to wait for the other to pass as the route was single track.

The great inventor and engineer was held back by the materials available for him to turn his grandiose scheme into reality. The hinge of the airtight valve and the ring around the piston were both made of leather, an organic material which was totally unsuitable for the purpose, but in the mid 19th century, no alternative material was available. Indeed, the Croydon line scrapped its atmospheric system after repeated breakdowns because of the failure of the valve, but Brunel notoriously failed to mention this to the South Devon board.

Instead, he appointed a large team of men to continually run a sticky sealant on the valve to make it airtight. The sealant was found to be non-effective after exposure to the air, so a new compound comprising cod-liver oil and soap was introduced, but fared no better.

The leather dried and cracked in the sun, wind and salty air, and famously, was said to have been gnawed away by rats, leaving air to leak in through the cracks. Accordingly, the stationary engines were required to work much harder and burn more coal to maintain the necessary pressure in the vacuum pipe.

Two miles of the valve had to be completely replaced, while at the same time the stationary steam engine pumps kept breaking down.

Eventually, the atmospheric railway functioned well. Nine trains a day ran between Exeter

Above left: Brunel's spectacular sea wall route needs colossal expenditure on maintenance to combat wave erosion which threatens to undermine the trackbed and cliff falls.

Above right: A 5in gauge working scale model of a Brunel atmospheric railway train built by Barometer World at Merton in North Devon, a firm whose business is based around the concept of air pressure!

and Teignmouth during the spring and summer of 1848, recording average speeds of 64mph. Passengers liked the trains, until those travelling third class were asked to get out and push when they broke down.

Yet the costs did not add up, and far from being a cheaper alternative to steam, the atmospheric was proving very expensive to run: it cost 37 pence per mile to run an atmospheric train compared to 16 pence for steam.

Angry directors tracked down the absent Brunel at his home in London's Duke Street. Brunel blamed the inventors of the system, and recommended the replacement of the pipes and the steam pumps.

However, with the railway having lost nearly £500,000, the board ordered the conversion of the line to steam haulage as from 10 September 1848. The route opened throughout as such on 2 April 1849.

The question remains – what if modern adequate materials had been available to Brunel? Would the atmospheric system have killed off steam a century before diesel and electric traction did?

A bizarre railway indeed. The other three lines built to the Clegg and Samuda system were similarly converted for much the same reasons.

Yet in hindsight, perhaps equally more bizarre was the coastal route which Brunel chose, leaving the railway at the mercy of high tides and storm surges not to mention cliff falls.

The public today love traveling over the route between Exeter and Newton Abbot because of its unsurpassed coastal scenery: it has been described as the most beautiful rail route in Britain, but is the most expensive part of the national rail network to maintain, with regular stoppages and delays.

Because of global warming and rising sea levels, there are regular calls to build an alterative route from Exeter to Plymouth, maybe reopening the Southern Railway main line via Okehampton and Tavistock. The GWR, which used the Teign Valley branch as a diversionary route when necessary from 1903 onwards, announced a scheme for an avoiding line in 1936, even buying land and marking out the route, but the plans were sunk by World War Two and never revived.

Brunel stretched engineering to the limits of his day and then went another mile, and spectacular though his achievement with the South Devon Railway route may be, Network Rail has been left counting the cost more than 150 years after his death.

And to return to my original analogy, at the time of writing, I have five different-sized vacuum cleaners around my house, but I still don't know anyone with the wall cavity version.

Out of three surviving pumping stations, two were never used. One is at Torre in Torquay, intended to serve a branch line, and the other is next to Totnes station, also never reached by the atmospheric system. Pictured is the Totnes pump house, part of a derelict dairy, which was saved when English Heritage listed it in 2008 following a massive local outcry against imminent demolition.

CHAPTER SEVEN

SPARKS AT THE SEASIDE: SHIP AHOY!

FOR TWO CENTURIES or more, Brighton has undoubtedly been Britain's fun resort, and in being so, has both knowingly and unwittingly contributed to the nation's good.

Isambard Kingdom Brunel, was sent there to recuperate after narrowly escaping death when the Thames Tunnel, then still under construction, flooded on 12 January 1828, killing six workmen. He spent several months convalescing in Brighton, but his recovery proved slow. When it was discovered that 22-year-old Isambard was having "exertions with actresses," he was sent to the more refined Bristol; suburb of Clifton to resume his convalescence. While there, he won a competition to design a suspension bridge over the Avon Gorge, sparking off a chain of events which led to him being chosen as engineer for the Great Western Railway…

A second railway revolution was literally sparked off in Brighton, right on the beach.

Inventor Magnus Volk, born at 35 (now 40) Western Road, Brighton on 19 October 1851, and who in 1879 demonstrated the town's first telephone link and became the first resident to install electricity in his home at 38 Dyke Road the year afterwards, built a new kind of railway along the seafront.

On 4 August 1883, he unveiled a quarter-mile-long 2ft gauge electric railway running from a site opposite the town's aquarium to the Chain Pier. Power was provided by a 2hp Otto gas engine driving a Siemans D5 50V DC generator. A small electric car with a 1½hp motor had a top speed of 6mph. Volk did not invent the electric railway: it was a Scotsman, Robert Davidson of Aberdeen, who built the first known electric locomotive in 1837.

The world's first electric passenger train was demonstrated by Werner von Siemens in Berlin in 1879. Its locomotive was driven by a 2.2 kW motor which picked up power from a third-rail supply. Two years later, Siemens opened the world's first electric tram line in Lichterfelde near Berlin.

Volk's ingenuity was in reimporting the concept to Britain in a workable and commercial format. He extended his line eastwards from the Aquarium to the Banjo Groyne, and the Arch at Paston Place to provide workshop and power facilities, widening the track to 2ft 8½in gauge, and producing two larger and more powerful passenger cars.

The enlarged 1400 yard-long line opened on 4 April 1884, with a passing loop in the middle. The line hugged the shoreline, using timber trestles to cross gaps in the shingle, and

The official opening of Volk's Electric Railway on 3 August 1883.

Magnus Volk, who reintroduced the electric railway concept to Britain after a Scotsman had invented it nearly half a century earlier.

The Brighton & Rottingdean Seaside Electric Railway's single car Pioneer *nicknamed* Daddy Long Legs.

Poster advertising both Brighton electric railways.

Volk's Electric Railway Car 9 passes through the carriage shed which spans the line near its midway point.

severe gradients to allow the cars to pass beneath the Chain Pier.

The public loved it, but Volk was angry at being refused permission to extend his line beyond the Banjo Groyne to Rottingdean, and so came up with a plan for a truly bizarre form of transport, a cross between a railway, a seaside pier and a ship.

The Brighton & Rottingdean Seashore Electric Railway consisted of two parallel 2ft 8½in gauge tracks, billed as 18ft gauge, the measurement between the outermost rails. The tracks were laid on concrete sleepers mortised into the bedrock.

This single car was a 45ft by 22ft pier-like structure which stood on four 23ft-long legs and weighed 45 tons and was powered by electric motor, current being supplied from an overhead pick-up with masts mounted at regular intervals in the sea..

Officially named *Pioneer*, but many called it *Daddy Long-Legs*. It needed not only a driver, but a qualified sea captain. Unlike any other train, it was also provided with lifeboats.

This 'railway in the sea' was officially opened on 28 November 1896, only to be severely damaged by a storm a week later, when *Pioneer* was turned on to its side.

Repairs completed, it reopened in July 1897, but Volk literally found himself swimming against the tide, for the prevailing current proved too powerful for *Pioneer*, and he could not afford to boost its power.

In 1900, the local council decided to build a beach protection barrier, and told Volk to divert his line around it. No finance was available, and so the line closed down. Some of the foundations of it can still be made out at low tide.

Volk finally obtained permission to extend his original electric railway to Black Rock and the new stretch opened in September 1901. Sadly, this was cut back again in 1930 when the council built a new swimming pool.

A new Black Rock station was opened on 7 May 1937 when Volk, then 85, took joint control of Car 10 for a journey. It was his last public appearance as he died peacefully at home 13 days later.

Since 1995, the line, now in the ownership of Brighton City Council (the local authority having taken it over in 1938), has been supported by local enthusiasts under the banner of the Volk's Electric Railway Association, who on special days run the trains themselves.

Volk's Electric Railway was not the first in the world to run on electricity, but the earlier ones have long since passed into history, and it was the first in Britain. Therefore of profound historical importance, Britain's electrified main line and underground railways today can legitimately trace an ancestry back to it, and as such it is a national treasure, even though uninformed passers-by might dismiss it as another seafront novelty from yesteryear.

Magnus Volk has also been immortalised in Brighton's Hollywood-style Walk of Fame, the brainchild of local resident David Courtney, the man who discovered pop star Leo Sayer in the seventies.

The Brighton terminus of the unique sea railway/ship on stilts.

Volk's Electric Railway Cars 7 and 8, repainted in 2008 in the line's maroon and cream 125th anniversary livery.

Rough Sea over Electric Railway, Brighton.

The Volk's Electric Railway trestle sections were often hit by storms. The shingle is now much higher and shields the line.

A service train on the Hythe Pier Railway.

Another unique pioneer electric railway worthy of mention is also to be found on the south coast.

The 2ft gauge Hythe Pier Railway runs the length of the 700-yard Hythe Pier, which links the Hampshire village of Hythe to the deep water channel of Southampton Water.

The railway probably dates from the opening of the pier in 1881 when it was used for transporting goods, and until 1922, wagons were pushed by hand.

The line was then rebuilt and electrified at 250V DC using third-rail pick-up.

Two four-wheel electric locomotives built by Brush (works numbers 16302 and 16307 of 1917), were originally used at the wartime mustard gas factory in Avonmouth. Built as battery-powered locomotives, they were converted to third-rail electric to run on the pier and renumbered No 1 and 2.

There are four bogie passenger cars, two having a driving cab at the seaward end, with the locomotive always positioned at the landward end.

The railway also has a four-wheel oil tank car to carry fuel to the Hythe ferries.

Each train connects at the pier head with an arrival and departure of the Hythe Ferry, which has its Southampton terminal at the Town Quay. A ferry has operated on this route since Tudor times.

The ferry and train run every half-hour seven days a week, with evening services operated on Thursday, Friday and Saturday. The railway may seem, and in fact is, something of a transport antique, but nonetheless carries more than 500,000 passengers a year. To make the same journey by road involves a seven-mile U-turn running the gauntlet of peak-hour bottlenecks, and as congestion worsens, so the Hythe Pier Railway is an increasingly important part of local public transport.

CHAPTER EIGHT
THE STEAM ENGINES THEY COULDN'T SCRAP!

BY THE EARLY SIXTIES, the days of steam haulage on the national network were numbered. The Western Region was among the first constituent parts of British Railways to implement modernisation with a fleet of diesel hydraulic locomotives, some types of which barely outlived the steam engines they superseded.

Yet in the heart of Cornwall, three engines which had been destined for the scrapyard before Queen Victoria died were still providing an essential service in the year that the Beatles had their first chart entry.

The three London & South Western Railway Class 0298 Beattie 2-4-0 well tanks had become legendary amongst enthusiasts in the fifties and early sixties, who trekked from far and wide to photograph them in action on the Padstow-Wadebridge-Bodmin route, and its Wenfordbridge mineral branch – which they had made their own.

It was purely because of the Wenford line that they had time and time again escaped the cutter's torch. Because of their short wheelbase, they were perfect for negotiating the sharp curves and gradients as the line twisted and turned in the wooded Camel valley up to the western edge of Bodmin Moor and the Wenford clay works.

Their story began in 1834, the year that Trevithick died, and when the Bodmin & Wadebridge Railway became the first in his home county to use steam locomotives. The line was intended to carry sand from the Camel estuary to inland farms for use as fertiliser. Its main line ran from Wadebridge to Wenfordbridge, with a branch to Bodmin,

The 1840s was the age of 'Railway Mania', and the LSWR, seeking to expand its empire, bought the Bodmin & Wadebridge with the aim of building a line through North Cornwall to link it to London. In this way, the LSWR was competing with the Great Western Railway, which was aiming to reach Penzance via the Cornwall Railway.

However, the Bodmin & Wadebridge, which was legally absorbed by the LSWR in 1888, remained an unconnected outpost until 1 June 1895, when it was finally joined to the LSWR via the North Cornwall Railway at Wadebridge. Seven years earlier, the Bodmin & Wadebridge had been connected to another line, not part of the LSWR system but to the rival GWR, which had opened a branch to Bodmin and Boscarne Junction.

Meanwhile, back in the 1860s, LSWR locomotive engineer Joseph Beattie had designed

LSWR 0298 class 2-4-0WT No 30587 at the modern-day Boscarne Junction, where the GWR once met its rival the LSWR, and which is now part of the Bodmin & Wenford Railway.

The third Beattie well tank which did not make it into preservation after final withdrawal, No 30586, at Wadebridge alongside GWR small prairie tank No 4569.

the Standard Well Tanks for use on London suburban duties. The design had its origins in the Nile class of 2-4-0 well tanks introduced in 1859, but were modified by Beyer Peacock in collaboration with the LSWR.

Apart from three constructed at Nine Elms, the entire class of 85 well tanks was built by Beyer Peacock at Gorton Works, between 1863 and 1877.

Increasing traffic loads rendered them largely obsolete within two decades.

The introduction of Adams 4-4-2 'radial' tanks in 1883 saw the need for the well-tanks in the London area greatly reduced. A dozen were withdrawn in the late 1880s, and under Beattie's successor William Adams, 31 were given tenders to convert them to 2-4-0s. The Adams O2 class 0-4-4 tanks also rendered more of the well tanks obsolete, and by the late 1890s, extinction for the type was looming.

The LSWR hit upon the idea of using the Beattie tanks on the tightly-curving Wenford line, and two years before the North Cornwall Railway arrived at Wadebridge, one of them, No 248, was despatched by sea to the town to replace the tired resident Fletcher Jennings 0-4-0 saddle tank *Bodmin*. By 1895, Nos 44, 266 and 298 were also in action on the Cornish lines.

Just three well tanks were left in 1895, all at Wadebridge: No 298 (later BR 30587) and No 314 (30585), which dated from 1874, and No 329 (30586) which was built in 1875.

The then LSWR mechanical engineer Dugald Drummond wanted them scrapped in 1900, when the type was considered well past its sell-by date, but an inspector who was so impressed with their condition and performance on Wenfordbridge duties persuaded the company otherwise, and they soldiered on.

Beattie well tanks Nos 30587 and 30585 double head back on home territory as they pass West Heath Road on the Bodmin & Wenford Railway on 12 October 2008.

By 1921, the boilers of the trio were almost worn out, and by rights they should have been scrapped. Again, the design was matchless for Wenford operations, and so three new boilers of the 1907 Drummond O2 pattern were built, with Nos 298 and 329 receiving injectors.

Another attempt to replace the Beatties came in 1929 when the SECR P class 0-6-0s were considered for use on the line. One of them, No 558, was trialled, but the track was damaged by its longer wheelbase: as a result, No 329, which had been condemned earned a reprieve.

Two years later, No 314 was found to have fractured frames, but because it could not be replaced, it was rebuilt with modified frames, and Nos 298 and 329 later followed suit.

They carried on through nationalisation and well into British Railways days: their last general repair was in 1960 when they received their BR classification 0P. By then, they were a real anachronism on the national network: they had been designed a century before and looked every year of it.

Old timers meet old timers: Beattie well tank no 248 in its early days at Bodmin.

In 1962, boundary changes saw the Western Region take control of the line from the Southern Region, and finally, the Beatties were replaced, at first by three 1369 class 0-6-0 pannier tanks, and then, in 1964, by Class 08 diesel shunters.

Two of them, Nos 30587 and 30587, were hired to run a series of farewell trips back in their native London.

A tour on 2 December 1962 tour saw the pair double head between Waterloo, Point Pleasant Junction, East Putney, Wimbledon, Surbiton, Hampton Court Junction and Hampton Court on their first run, before taking their six-coach special to Wimbledon and its yard. H16 class 4-6-2T No 30517 then joined the programme, taking the train on a return trip from Wimbledon yard to Chessington South.

The Beatties took over again, running together from Wimbledon yard to Shepperton and on to Waterloo. Due to heavy demand, the tour was repeated on 16 December when the train ran from Waterloo to Wimbledon, before No 30517 stepped in for a return trip to Chessington South. The Beatties' final leg was from Wimbledon via Shepperton, where the train reversed, to Strawberry Hill, Twickenham, and finally to Waterloo.

Incidentally, it was not the only time one of them had been away from Cornwall during their 70 years service there. In 1955, No 30587 worked a Railway Enthusiasts Club special from Andover Junction to Bulford Camp and back, heading a LSWR three-coach non-corridor set.

No 30585 hauls a vintage train at its Buckinghamshire Railway Centre home.

Because of its historical importance, No 30587 was officially designated for preservation at part of the National Collection in 1961, and its future was assured.

The London Railway Preservation Society, which evolved into the Quainton Railway Society, operator of today's Buckinghamshire Railway Centre, eventually bought No 30585, which by then had clocked up 1,314,838 miles in 89 years of service. Sadly, No 30586 was scrapped, but the society obtained several parts for use with No 30585.

No 30585 was steamed for the first time in preservation on 22 March 1970, but withdrawn two years later for overhaul, and the beginning of long-term restoration. It was, however, able to resteam in the mid-seventies with a new boiler ticket and ran until it was again withdrawn in the eighties.

No 30587 later found itself repainted into LSWR green and displayed inside the South Devon Railway's museum at Buckfastleigh.

The Bodmin Road-Bodmin General-Padstow route closed to passengers on 30 January 1967, but the line was retained for freight as far as Wadebridge until December 1978, and the Wenford branch remained open for china clay traffic from Wenford dries to Bodmin Road (now Bodmin Parkway) until September 1983. Shortly afterwards, preservationists began moves to save the Bodmin Parkway-Wenford line. The Parkway-Bodmin General-Boscarne Junction line has been reborn as the Bodmin & Wenford Railway, but plans to reinstate the lifted Wenford freight branch were blocked by a legal challenge from some local residents in 1997, and today it forms part of the Camel Trail long-distance cyclepath.

A knight in shining white armour subsequently appeared for both locomotives, in the form of retired London banker Alan Moore. He undertook his National Service in Bodmin in 1955 and had fond memories of the line having regularly ridden over it in its Western Region days.

No 30587 recreates a Wenfordbridge branch cameo scene at Sir William McAlpine's private Fawley Hill Railway in Berkshire.

He had played a pivotal role in the development of the Bodmin & Wenford Railway through its charitable supporting trust, and has been the line's major financial benefactor.

He persuaded the National Railway Museum, custodians of No 30587, to allow it to be removed from Buckfastleigh and sponsored its rebuild to operational condition at the Flour Mill Colliery workshop at Bream in the Forest of Dean, a leading modern-day steam locomotive restoration base established in the 1990s by chartered surveyor Bill Parker.

No 30587 triumphantly returned to steam at Bodmin in autumn 2002, and subsequently, the Moore-Parker team tackled No 30585, the former sponsoring the completion of its overhaul, at the latter's workshop.

The latter was resteamed on 7 October 2006 at Quainton, with an official relaunch by Sir William McAlpine. A week later No 30585 left for Bodmin, as part of the restoration agreement, where it was reunited with No 30587 on 'home' territory for the first time since 1962.

The pair have since run together both at Bodmin and Quainton Road.

Amongst the greatest of all steam locomotive survivors still in regular service, they provide an invaluable window on the world of mid-Victorian railways and locomotive practices. If only that wonderful Wenford line had survived too!

CHAPTER NINE
NEW ROOM AT THE TOP

AT THE SAME TIME as inventing the steam railway locomotive, Richard Trevithick also invented the steam-hauled rack railway. Britain gave this invention to the rest of the world, where it has been used to magnificent effect, and it yet made use of it only in one instance – the Snowdon Mountain Railway.

Trevithick had originally built steam-powered road vehicles, turning to rail because the poor roads of the day could not hold them. Rail was not the whole answer, as the weight of the locomotives often cracked the rails on which they ran, as happened with his first public demonstration of a steam engine at the Penydarren Tramroad in 1804.

Trevithick believed that the friction of metal wheels on metal rails would be too low for a substantial weight to be pulled without the engine slipping. To counter this problem, his first experimental locomotives were built with teeth on the wheels on one side, which engaged in teeth on the corresponding rails. Although it was a case of technological overkill, as it was not needed on slight gradients, the cog or rack railway concept had been born.

The first cog railway in the world was the Middleton Railway at Leeds, which has operated continuously since 1758, and which installed a rack and pinion system in 1812 when it upgraded from horse power to steam traction.

At Clogwyn, the Snowdon Mountain Railway is laid along a ridge, giving stupendous views of the glaciated landscape around and below.

Developing Trevithick's ideas, the Middleton system was patented by John Blenkinsop in 1811. Indeed, what is said to be the first commercial steam locomotive in the world, the *Salamanca*, ran along it in 1812. The weight and friction needed to be kept low to stop the locomotive breaking the brittle cast iron rails.

It was the Americans, not the Swiss as you might suppose, who were the first to apply the cog railway concept to a mountain line. The Mount Washington Cog Railway in New Hampshire, using a central rack system designed by Sylvester Marsh, opened for passengers in 1868. Three years later, it was followed by the Vitznau-Rigi-Bahn on Mount Rigi in Switzerland, the first

37

No 5 Moel Siabod, one of the first batch of locomotives ordered from Switzerland, because no British manufacturer could be found.

Completely open to the elements: a train comprising one of the original coaches en route to Summit station. The first carriages were open above the waist and their canvas curtains provided scant protection against the elements, but between 1951 and 1957, they were rebuilt with enclosed bodies.

mountain rack railway on the continent, which used the rack system developed by Niklaus Riggenbach.

Riggenbach employed Swiss locomotive engineer Roman Abt, who came up with a cheaper rack system with simpler pointwork, and based on fixing solid bars mounted centrally between the rails with vertical offset teeth machined into them. This made sure that the pinions on the locomotive's driving wheels are constantly engaged with the rack, while the pinion wheels can be mounted on the same axle as the rail wheels.

This is the system that can be seen today on Mount Snowdon.

At first sight, most visitors are amazed by the steam locomotives on rack railways being built at an angle, with their boilers facing down. Steam engines can operate only when the boiler is level, because water must cover the boiler tubes and firebox sheets at all times, if an almighty explosion is to be avoided. Often, the entire rack railway, including engine sheds, has to be built on a slope to accommodate such locomotives: many continental rack railways nowadays used modern traction, as diesel and electric locomotives do not have the same problem.

A proposal to build a cog railway to the top of Snowdon, the highest peak in England and Wales, emerged in 1869, as tourist numbers arriving at Llanberis via the London & North Western Railway's branch from Caernarfon soared, but principal objector and landowner George William Duff Assheton-Smith said it would spoil the magnificent mountain views. Supported by nature lovers, he said that if anyone wanted to climb Snowdon, there was a perfectly-adequate rough track available.

A different approach was taken when the 1ft 11½ gauge North Wales Narrow Gauge Railway (later the Welsh Highland Railway) began running past the far side of the mountain, with a station called South Snowdon, and Llanberis traders worried they would miss out.

The Snowdon Mountain Tramway and Hotel Company was formed – with George Assheton-Smith as its chairman following a road to Damascus conversion – to build the railway, an Act of Parliament being unnecessary as it was to be constructed wholly on private land. Used the Abt rack system, it was to be built to 2ft 7½in gauge, running four miles 1188 yards with an average gradient of 1-in-7.86 as it rises from 353ft above sea level at Llanberis to 3493ft at Summit station, the steepest section being 1-in5.5, with two substantial viaducts being between Llanberis and Waterfall. Intitially, it was hoped that the railway would carry freight as well as passengers, serving the needs of farmers whose sheep grazed on the slopes!

Enid Assheton-Smith, a member of the landowner's family, cut the first sod in December 1894. It was completed in February 1896, at a cost of £63,800. At first, it had seven stations, including the first up the line from Llanberis, Waterfall, which is now closed.

At Clogwyn station, 2556ft above sea level, the wind speed is measured to assess whether it is safe for trains to proceed on to Summit station, which lies just 68ft below the 3560ft mountain peak. If not, they stop at Rocky Valley Halt.

The Swiss Locomotive and Machine Works of Winterthur was awarded the contract to build the first five Snowdon engines, 0-4-2Ts Nos 1 to 5, with three more, Nos 6-8, following in 1922/23.

The line was officially opened on Monday 6 April 1896, when two trains ran up to the summit.

On the first return trip down the mountain, locomotive No 1 *Ladas* (a name comprising the initials of George's wife Laura Alice Duff Assheton-Smith) with two carriages lost the rack on the 1-in5.5 gradient and ran out of control. The locomotive derailed and plunged down the steep side of the ravine to land upside down far below without its boiler, a total wreck.

A passenger, Ellis Griffith Roberts of Llanberis, died from blood loss after leaping from his carriage. The second downward train, hauled by No 2 *Enid*, collided with the derailed carriages of the first, but mercifully there were no more fatalities. There has never been a replacement No 1 on the railway.

An inquiry ruled that the cause of the accident was post-construction settlement, compounded by excess speed caused by the weight of the train. Afterwards, the maximum allowed train weight was reduced to the equivalent of one-and-a-half of the existing carriages. Subsequently lighter carriages were constructed so two-coach trains could operate again.

Furthermore, a gripper system, the only one in use on any Abt system line, was installed to boost adhesion on the rack.

The locomotives always push the carriages, for reasons of safety. The carriages are left uncoupled to the locomotive, because gravity will always push the vehicle down against the locomotive. In turn, the engines are fitted with powerful brakes that grip the rack rail solidly.

An early view of Llanberis station with No 4 Snowdon *waiting to depart.*

No 7 Ralph Sadler *being maintained at Llanberis workshops. Note the sloping boiler.*

The final climb to the summit.

The 1935 Summit station terminus and hotel.

The railway reopened on 9 April 1897, and there have been no fatalities since.

In 1935, a new summit station was built, designed by Sir Clough Williams-Ellis, who designed the Italianate village of Portmeirion near Porthmadog. Architecturally, his somewhat utilitarian station came in for a pasting in recent times from critics, including the Prince of Wales who called it "the highest slum in Wales".

The Ministry of Supply undertook experimental radio work at Summit station in 1942, and a passenger service was run despite wartime cutbacks. In 1943, the RAF requisitioned the Summit Hotel as an experimental radar station, running passenger trains as a decoy.

The Admiralty then took over the hotel to work on the refinement of radar techniques, and while public trains still ran, no member of the public was allowed into the building.

When services fully resumed after World War Two, coal was in such short supply that old army boots were instead burned in the engines' fireboxes.

The line's first two diesel locomotives were financed by a share issue in 1985, and two more, also built by Hunslet, followed. Three railcars built by HPE Tredegar Ltd were also added to the fleet.

A modern replacement for the despised Summit terminus was officially opened by Welsh Assembly First Minister Rhodri Morgan on 12 June 2009. Named Hafod Eryri, Welsh for "high residence of Snowdonia" and cost £8.4-million, largely made up of grant aid and public donations. The railway played a part in its construction, by carrying building materials, and therefore at long last running real freight trains in the process.

As expected, the railway is a costly operation, with 24 of the 50 full-time staff dedicated to engineering, including 11 on track maintenance.

Hafod Eryri, the new Summit station building, which opened in 2009

Passenger trains depart from Llanberis at up to every 30 minutes at busy times, and in the peak summer season, are often sold out.

The first movement of the day is the works train which ferries supplies, including drinking water and fuel for the generator, to Summit station, as well as provisions for the café at Halfway station, and also carries the permanent way maintenance gang.

In 2010, the railway appointed its first female guard in 19-year-old Rachel Owen from Bangor, who said it was fulfilling a lifetime's ambition. "Being up there in charge of a train with the drivers is an amazing feeling," she said.

CHAPTER TEN
WIND POWER!

RAILWAYS ARE OFTEN hailed as 'green' transport because they in theory have the power to replace cars and lorries off roads and reduce exhaust emissions from road vehicles.

However, modern railways do leave a carbon footprint. Diesel locomotives emit exhaust fumes too, and electric trains are likely to obtain their current from coal-fired power stations, if nuclear or renewable alternatives are not available. And what could be more renewable than wind power?

What's more, could it be used to power a train?

Surveyor and engineering consultant Charles Easton Spooner in 1856 became manager of the Festiniog Railway, a line which he is said to have helped survey in 1830 at the age of 12. There, he also acted as engineer, company secretary, engineer and locomotive superintendent. He was awarded a gold medal by the Tsar of Russia following the 1870 trials on the line of Robert Fairlie's double Fairlie locomotive *Little Wonder*.

A great innovator himself, in 1872 Spooner introduced bogie carriages on the Festiniog Railway. They were the world's first iron-framed bogie carriages.

In 1878, a three-masted Porthmadog-built schooner was named after him. That was indeed appropriate, for Charles clearly loved boats so much that he had one built to run on the railway itself!

Resembling a traditional rowing boat on wheels, it was powered only by a large sail and served as Spooner's personal inspection saloon.

Today's health and safety experts would have had fits if they had seen it in operation on the line. Their fears would have been fully justified, for 'The Boat', as it was known, came to grief when it was destroyed on 12 February 1886 in a head-

The modern-day replica of Charles Spooner's Festiniog Railway inspection saloon 'The Boat'.

The lifeboatmen's sail bogie in use on the Spurn Head Railway.

Another view of a Spurn Head sail bogie.

on collision with an up passenger train, Spooner having taken possession of the single-line staff before sailing ahead.

When the modern-day Ffestiniog Railway former archivist Michael Seymour died in 1998, he left a legacy specifically for the building of a replica of 'The Boat'.

In the years that followed, staff at the line's Boston Lodge Works began work on the project, although they had no plans to work on.

All that existed was an engraving, a textual description which alluded to the boat-like prow, and a single photograph of Tanybwlch. Nonetheless, a design was produced with help from professional boatbuilders.

Bill Piper, a Porthmadog boat builder, played a pivotal role in helping the carriage department's team build the new Spooner boat, which was completed in 2005.

While Spooner's boat was for his private use, elsewhere, sail craft on rails were used for travel by members of the public, in several places around Britain.

The best-known examples are the sail bogies which ran on the Spurn Head Railway, built during World War One as part of fortifications to guard the mouth of the Humber.

Spurn Head is the name given to the distinctive narrow sand spit that reaches across the mouth of the River Humber from its northern bank as it enters the North Sea. The spit has changed position many times during the course of history due to natural forces of coastal erosion and is built up of sand and shingle washed down from as far away as Flamborough Head.

As part of the defences, two coastal artillery 9.2in batteries were added at either end of Spurn Head, with 4in and 4.7in quick-firing guns in between.

Much of the building materials were brought in by water, as access to Spurn Head by land involved a three-mile walk over sand dunes. To speed up the processs, the War Department decided to add its own railway to bring both men and materials to the new fortress at Spurn Head.

Contractor CJ Wills of Manchester brought five tank engines to build the line, one staying on afterwards to operate it.

The standard gauge line ran from a northern terminus at Kilnsea, at a fort named Godwin Battery, for 3¾ miles to Green Battery at Spurn Point, where an engine shed was built just north of the lighthouse. The contractors also built a railway pier near the tip of Spurn Head, complete with steam crane, to receive building materials brought in by river.

One of three Hudswell Clarke 0-4-0 saddle tanks used to build the line, No 402 of 1893 *Lord Mayor*, survived into preservation, and is now part of the Vintage Carriages Trust collection at the Museum of Rail Travel at Ingrow on the Keighley & Worth Valley Railway.

Several petrol-engined railcars, all but one made by Drewery, were introduced from 1920 onwards.

However, the railway's most unusual and unforgettable feature was the use of two sail

All aboard a Spurn Head 'land ship'!

bogies or trolleys which emerged during World War One. The earliest recorded use of a sail trolley was in 1915.

They were wooden platforms with flanged wheels, similar to the type once commonly used by platelayers, but with a mast fixed in the centre, to which a large balanced lug sail was fixed and braced to the corners of the trolley.

They were built and used both by the Spurn Head lifeboatmen and the men working for the War Department, who offered trips on them to visitors. No seats were provided and passengers had to sit directly on the decking.

The sail bogies had no brakes and they were stopped by dropping a heavy piece of timber in front of the wheels.

It is said that the sail bogies could reach a reasonable speed, but if the wind was too fierce, they would blow over. On calmer days, the sail bogie had to be pushed by hand – highlighting the fact that they had not quite managed to supersede steam or internal combustion power!

Nevertheless, the sail bogies proved preferable to walking all the way to and from Kilnsea. The military's sail bogie was often used to check that the line was clear of sand drifts.

But it was not all plain sailing for the bogies.

On one occasion, a group of soldiers who had been drinking at the Blue Bell Inn in Kilnsea boarded the trolley, hoisted the sail, and set off for Spurn Point. They all fell asleep while in transit, just as wind picked up.

The engine sheds pictured in 1952 after the line was closed.

Spurn Head, the great shifting sandspit across the mouth of the Humber.

South Carolina Railroad's sailcar, as seen in a contemporary sketch.

Speeding towards the southern terminus, one of the soldiers woke in time to realise their peril. He just managed to stop the sail bogie ramming the battery entrance gates.

Another time, a sail bogie went to Kilnsea to collect a married couple. It rapidly gathered speed on the way back and when it reached 40mph the inexperienced man in charge panicked and jumped off. The husband instructively followed him, but his wife stayed on the trolley, suffering cuts to her face. Luckily the wind dropped and the bogie slowed down before the fort was reached.

The Reverend Alfred Poulsom, Methodist chaplain at Spurn Point, recorded that a sail bogie once powered towards a coastguard who was walking on the track not only with his back to the oncoming vessel but who was completely oblivious to it. The sail was lowered to no effect, and then the 'brake' was dropped in front of the bogie - which was travelling at such a speed that it cut straight through the block without stopping. However, the noise alerted the coastguard who leaped clear with seconds to spare.

The military sail bogie was later fitted with a Raleigh 350cc side valve engine and gearbox, but it was wrecked on its trial run when it ended up under a railway truck due to wrongly-set points.

Records are sketchy, but it is believed that sail power was last used on the railway during World War Two, or just afterwards.

The railway was finally declared redundant in the winter of 1951-52 after which Sheffield contractor Thomas W Ward Ltd ripped up the line. The Spurn Head military establishments were decommissioned between 1956-59. Since 1960, Spurn Head has been owned by the Yorkshire Wildlife Trust and is a designated National Nature Reserve and, Heritage Coast and is part of the Humber Flats, Marshes and Coast Special Protection Area.

Traces of the line to be seen today: at three points, rails are still embedded in the concrete road, while a short section of track remains inside what was the entrance to the Spurn battery.

Elsewhere, the Francis Alpha cement works at Cliffe on the Isle of Grain in Kent had a railway linking it to a quay a mile away, and a sail trolley was used on it to inspect sea defences.

A sail trolley was built by agricultural and construction machinery manufacturer Ransomes & Rapier for use at its Waterside Works in Ipswich in 1869. Another ran on a railway at South Gare in Teesside, while one operated on the military railway between Fort Blockhouse and Fort Monckton in Gosport, Hampshire, around 1895.

In the early 20th century, the Admiralty Wireless Tramway at Port Stanley in the Falkland Islands used several sail trolleys.

Sadly, Britain probably cannot claim a world first here, for a sail-powered carriage was sketched in action on the South Carolina Railroad in 1829, the same year as the USA's first steam locomotive, the British-built *Stourbridge Lion*, was first steamed.

CHAPTER ELEVEN
NOWHERE TO RUN

IN THE WAKE OF the Industrial Revolution, steam railways not only brought multiple benefits to the world, but created the modern age. Before the coming of the railways, for instance, every town in the country had its own local time zone, which could vary greatly from that of the capital. The arrival of the railway with train guards equipped with their watches meant that Greenwich Mean Time could become standard.

Yet back in the 1820s, there was no national railway network, telephone, no internet, no swift means of communication between the early railway pioneers other than writing letters or meeting face to face. Therefore a railway engineer in south-west England might well be totally oblivious to the finer points of what his counterpart would be doing in the Durham coalfield, including the question of gauge.

Today, the entire locomotive fleet of South Devon's Lee Moor Tramway survives. Not many heritage railways can make such a boast, but in the Lee Moor's case, it amounted to just a pair of Peckett 0-4-0 saddle tanks. Splendid locomotives they were and still are, and for a very reasonable amount of money, they could be returned to working order after an absence of more than 60 years.

However, no railway today exists on which they could run as they are. For they were built to the local 'Dartmoor gauge' of 4ft 6in – which means that for the sake of 2½ins, they must remain as static museum exhibits, unless someone provides the money for a short demonstration line to be laid.

The Lee Moor Tramway was famous for its flat crossing of the Great Western Railway's London-Penzance four-track main line at Laira Junction near Plymouth. In railway technology terms, it was almost a case of stone age man meets space age.

With wooden boards laid between the rails to prevent them tripping, horses would haul short rakes of china clay wagons across the busy tracks which were the domain of Kings, Castles and other illustrious express passenger locomotives.

There could never be a physical junction between the two lines, because the Lee Moor boasted the widest narrow gauge track of all.

The 4ft 6in track gauge dates back to the distant times before anyone even dreamed about Paddington-Penzance by train, let alone a national railway network laid to the 4ft 8½in gauge

Peckett No 2 inside its previous home in a small museum at Saltram House near Plymouth. Last steamed on 31 December 1945, it is now part of the South Devon Railway collection at Buckfastleigh.

A horse hauls a rake of china clay wagons over the Lee Moor Tramway's boarded level crossing with the GWR main line at Laira Junction in 1930. This picture is taken from Images of Industrial & Narrow Gauge Railways – Devon, *by Maurice Dart, and also published by Halsgrove.*

Peckett No 1 at the Wheal Martyn China Clay Museum near St Austell.

devised in the north east by a colliery engineman named George Stephenson.

Sir Thomas Tyrwhitt, who built Prince's Town (Princetown) in the heart of the Dartmoor and named it after the Prince of Wales, later King George IV, also suggested to the Admiralty that a prisoner-of-war camp to house captured Napoleonic soldiers could be built there, and so Dartmoor Prison was completed in 1809. When peace broke out in 1815, the prison emptied, and Tyrwhitt looked to rail as a means of reclaiming the moor as farmland and transporting granite from local quarries.

What was the first railway to link Plymouth to another town, running from the city's Sutton Pool harbour 25 miles to Princetown, opened on 26 September 1823, and was named the Plymouth & Dartmoor Railway. At that time, Stephenson was still working on the Hetton Railway, the world's first purpose-designed line for steam haulage, and nobody in deepest Devon could have been expected to foresee a time when his 4ft 8½in gauge would become the norm. So Tyrwhitt chose the rounded figure of 4ft 6in which admirably suited his purpose. It became known as 'Dartmoor gauge'

In 1883, the top section of his railway north of Yelverton was converted to standard gauge as the Princetown branch, and later became part of the GWR portfolio.

The rest of Tyrwhitt's 4ft 6in gauge railway fell into disuse around 1900, and most of it was lifted by 1916.

The Lee Moor Tramway was a privately-owned mineral railway that was built to carry china clay and other produce from the south-western edge of Dartmoor to Sutton Harbour, and used the Plymouth & Dartmoor Railway track for the lower portion of its journey. It was also built to Dartmoor gauge.

Lord Morley, who owned the mineral rights at Lee Moor, where rich deposits of china clay had been found, leased them to J&W Phillips in September 1833. After several schemes came to nothing, work on building a railway to carry the extracted clay, a product of rotting granite, to the quayside began in 1853. This first line was badly constructed and in June 1856 Lord Morley and Phillips obtained the right to run their own china clay traffic to Plymouth – as long as the 4ft 6in gauge remained – and rebuilt the tramway to operational standards, including its viaduct at Wotter and the great incline at Torycombe.

The tramway was officially reopened on 24 September 1858. By then, the 7ft 0¼in Brunel gauge South Devon Railway had bought the Plymouth & Dartmoor Railway's Sutton Harbour branch and converted it to dual gauge, so trains from both systems could run over it.

The Lee Moor Tramway was operated by horses until 1899, when the saddle tanks were ordered from Peckett of Bristol to cope with a surge in clay traffic. The line was upgraded to accommodate them and an engine shed built at Torycombe clay works They operated exclusively on the northern section above the 1¼-mile rope-worked 1-in-11 Cann incline; the line south of that point to Sutton Harbour including that famous flat crossing was worked by horses until the end.

Leemoor No 1 and *No 2*, the only 4ft 6in gauge locomotives ever built by Peckett, wore green livery yellow and green lining and dull red frames and wheels.

The closure of the tramway began as early as 1910 when the top part of the line from Lee Moor village to Cholwich Town pits was shut down. Torycombe incline closed in 1936, and the remainder of the line followed after the start of World War Two, only to be pressed back into service to carry naval stores moved from the heavily-bombed Royal Dockyard at Devonport to Lee Moor for safekeeping.

The tramway reopened properly on 8 October 1945 but closed again in 1947, leaving only the stretch from Marsh Mills to Maddocks Concrete Works at Laira, along which sand was conveyed in order to maintain the right-of-way across the GWR main line.

This crossing was used 14 times in 1958 but that dropped to six in 1959 and just four in 1960. The final crossing was made on 26 August 1960, at 11.19am on the outward journey and finally at 1.27pm when the horse and empty tracks returned towards Marsh Mills.

Rather than any downturn in traffic, it was the productivity of the Lee Moor pits that led to the demise of the tramway, which could not cope with the workload. It was ripped up and replaced with a pipeline above Marsh Mills, although the track remained in place between Marsh Mills and Laira. Today, a cyclepath follows much of the tramway across the moorland.

The Lee Moor Preservation Society, was formed in February 1964 by members of the Plymouth Railway Circle to preserve the two locomotives. No 2 was cosmetically restored for display at the National Trust's Saltram House at Plympton to where it was moved on 20 July 1970. No 1 went to the Wheal Martyn China Clay Museum near St Austell on 17 March 1975, by which time the society had been disbanded.

A horse train at the tramway's weighbridge in Longbridge, Plymouth. There were sometimes up to a dozen trucks a day pulled by horses down to the wharf at Sutton.

Built in 1934 to the extremely rare (in UK) metre gauge, the classic outlines of this 0-6-0 saddle tank betray its common ancestry with the Lee Moor pair, in that it was also manufactured by Peckett. It was supplied to Wellingborough Iron Company Ltd for use at Finedon Quarry, and eventually became Stewarts & Lloyds No 86. Despite having only a short demonstration line on which to run, it was returned to steam at Irchester in December 2002, having been preserved in 1967.

A picture unlikely to be repeated: Peckett No 1 in steam at Torycombe.

Pecketts Nos 1 and 2 taken outside the Torycombe engine shed on 18 May 1966 for the first time in more than 20 years.

In 2001, No 2 was moved the South Devon Railway at Buckfastleigh, where it is safely kept in a shed, with agreement reached for its sister engine to follow at a later date.

Steam returned to a tiny part of the Lee Moor line in 2009 when the Plym Valley Railway, a standard gauge heritage line from Marsh Mills which has been laid on part of the GWR Plymouth- Launceston route, was extended as far as the level crossing which took the tramway across it.

At this point I hate to spoil the fun of OO gauge modellers by reminding them that their layouts do not accurately reflect 4ft 8½in gauge. At 4mm to the foot, OO gauge track measures up to 4ft 1½in full size – a full 4½in narrower than the Lee Moor Tramway, and more akin to the 4ft Pardan Railway in Caernarfonshire. This bizarre but universally-accepted anomaly dates back to the launch of OO by Bing in 1921 as 'The Table Railway', running on 16.5mm track, accurate for HO which is 3.5mm to the foot, but scaling rolling stock, because the large miniature propulsion mechanisms back then could not fit into models of British prototypes which have a smaller loading gauge than their US or continental counterparts.

A problem similar to that faced by the two Lee Moor survivors exists at the Irchester Narrow Gauge Railway Museum near Wellingborough in Northamptonshire, where seven locomotives in the collection, including three classic Peckett 0-6-0 saddle tanks, are built to metre gauge. Used locally in the county's ironstone quarries, metre gauge is commonplace on the continent and in many other counties round the world, but extremely rare in Britain, where it was to be found in industrial applications, and the operational Irchester stock is limited to a 250-metre running line, with live steam demonstrations once a month during summer.

This in itself is a truly bizarre scenario, because what is believed to be the world's first metre-gauge line was laid at what is now the Crich Tramway Museum in Derbyshire in 1841 to serve a limestone quarry by none other than George Stephenson, he of 4ft 8½in gauge fame!

An unsubstantiated story runs that Stephenson, who spent the last ten years of his life in nearby Chesterfield, hired Dutch engineers to build 'a narrow gauge railway' but did not specify the exact gauge, so they simply chose the basic continental measurement. It is also said that one of the locomotives from Crich found its way to the Northamptonshire ironstone fields, and that a mineral railway was built to suit its albeit rare gauge.

However, at least the operational Irchester locomotives have somewhere to run, and in theory could operate abroad, whereas the Dartmoor gauge duo have nowhere.

CHAPTER TWELVE
THE SIAMESE TWINS OF STEAM

FOR MANY READERS, the most unforgettable railway featured in this book is to be found in County Kerry.

There, a short demonstration line has been built, together with a replica steam locomotive (but powered by a diesel engine), to recreate the legendary Listowel & Ballybunion Railway.

Above all else, the line was famous for its 'twin' steam locomotives, joined as if by the hip, and running on an A-shaped monorail trestle.

The system, known as a Lartigue monorail, was devised by French engineer Charles Lartigue, who came up with what was next to a completely new form of land transport.

Born in Toulouse in 1834, in his forties, he saw camels in Algeria carrying heavy loads across the desert, balanced in panniers on their backs.

His mind went into overdrive. Here was the futuristic railway system the world had been waiting for. Instead of locomotives and stock running on two rails fixed to the sleepers, why not have a single rail at waist height carried on trestles? The locomotives and rolling stock would then sit astride the track just like the camels' panniers.

By 1881, Lartigue had a 56-mile-long A-section monorail running across the Algerian desert, built to carry esparto grass. There was a genuine point to this venture, as the shifting sands of the desert would have made a conventional railway unusable.

While in the desert, an A-shaped monorail might be a resounding success, Lartigue somehow failed to grasp the point that the rest of the world was not neceesarily built on sand.

In 1886 he demonstrated his system in London in a bid to convince others it was better than the railways of the day. Yet if Brunel could not convince everyone his broad gauge was the best, what chance did Lartigue have?

Nonetheless, a demand from residents of North Kerry to be linked to the Irish railway network arrived at Westminster, and some bright spark seized the opportunity to test Lartigue's system by building a nine-mile line between Listowel and Ballybunion, the birthplace of Lord Kitchener, which had aspirations to become a major beach resort.

The railway cost £30,000 to build and opened on 1 March 1888, giving both towns instant international fame for being served by the world's first steam monorailway.

It was not a true monorail, as on each side of the trestle lay another rail, which carried

Builder's photograph of an original Listowel & Ballybunion Railway Hunslet 0-3-0.

The replica steam outline Listowel & Ballybunion locomotive encounters one of the points. The train travels at 15mph while on the main line, approximately the same speed as the originals.

A postcard view of the Listowel & Ballybunion Railway in 1900.

unpowered stabilising wheels fitted to all the engines and wagons to prevent them from overbalancing.

In October 1887, Leeds engine builder Hunslet supplied three engines to the line, designed by fabled articulated locomotive engineer Anatole Mallet. They were 0-6-0s – or rather, 0-3-0s. Looking like steam Siamese twins, they were specially built with two boilers in order to balance on the track, and therefore needed two fireboxes, one of which had to be stoked by the driver, the other in the time-honoured way by the fireman. It was said that the engines could haul a load of 240 tons at 30mph.

They also had powered tenders to give extra power when climbing gradients. The tender wheels were driven by two cylinders via spur gears, and a pair of small chimneys were fitted to each tender to discharge the steam from these cylinders.

Therefore, the Listowel & Ballybunion locomotives had a wheel arrangement of 0-3-0 + 0-2-0. However, the boilers could not generate enough steam to run the tender engines as well, and they were never used.

As well as passengers, the trains carried freight, cattle and sand from the beaches to use as fertiliser. Golfers travelled over the line to the then new course at Ballybunion which eventually became one of the best in the world.

Drawback time: freight loads had to be evenly balanced. If a farmer sent a cow to market

A Lartigue train leaving Listowel station.

via monorail, he would have to send two calves to balance it. They would travel back on opposite sides of the same freight wagon, thereby balancing each other. Similarly, passengers could not pass from one side of a carriage to another while the train was running.

Furthermore, it was impossible to build level crossings. When a road was encountered, a double-sided drawbridge had to be provided, with an attendant to operate it.

Where farmers' tracks crossed the line, level crossings took the form of a swivelling turntable, locked before and after use, with the farmer given a key.

Worse still, traditional railway points were out of the question, so more trestle-mounted turntables were needed to access sidings and passing loops.

Speaking plainly, the monorail design was workable, but ludicrous by comparison. Nonetheless, it just about managed to break even, and astonishingly, ran for 36 years.

Its demise came not, as might be expected, through competition from road transport, but because it was damaged during the Irish Civil War of 1921-23. The line closed in 1924 and everything was scrapped apart from a short section of track.

The Kerry line was not unique. After it opened, a 10-mile Lartigue line was built to serve Panissières in the Loire region of France, with two locomotives, named *Feurs* and *Panissières*. Tests in 1895/6 proved less than satisfactory, and the line was finally sold for scrap in 1902. A modern-day replica of a locomotive is displayed in Panissières.

Passengers crossing the tracks on a steps bogie. Some carriages had a footbridge built into the rear, so that when the train stopped at a station, they could alight, cross over the track and board the same coach from the other side. If they moved over while in transit, the coach might tip over!

Schoolgirls learn the finer points about the most bizarre passenger railway in the British Isles.

Lartigue died in 1907. The last Lartigue monorail was opened by the Sierra Salt Corporation in California's Mojave Desert in the mid-twenties. It worked well for two years, only for the mine to close.

In 1988, local politician Michael Guerin produced a history of the Kerry line to coincide with its centenary, while fellow Lartigue enthusiast Michael Barry had preserved 50 metres of salvaged track and an original carriage. Rekindled interest led to a campaign for at least part of the distinctive railway to be rebuilt as part of local heritage.

After a Lartigue Restoration Committee was established in the 1990s, English locomotive builder Alan Keef Ltd of Ross-on-Wye was asked to build a replica locomotive, but for ease of operation, to use a diesel motor. Keef was also contracted to construct a pair of third-class carriages.

In 2003, a 1000-metre section of Lartigue monorail on the trackbed of the former line was opened, complete with three points, a pair of turntables and three platforms representing Listowel, Lisselton and Ballybunion. The site of the original Lartigue station is preserved in a park next to the new monorail.

So passengers today can once again ride on what may well be considered the most bizarre public railway in the British Isles.

CHAPTER THIRTEEN
PLEASE MR POSTMAN

THE CARRIAGE OF mail by railways has played an integral part in the shaping of the modern world. Before the development of the national rail network, let alone telegraph services, stagecoaches could take several days to take a letter from one part of the country to another. Railways reduced that time to a matter of hours, with infinite benefits to society and the economy.

The carriage of mail dates from an agreement of 1830 between the General Post Office and the Liverpool & Manchester Railway, In 1838, the Railways (Conveyance of Mails) Act was passed, directing railway companies to carry mail, by ordinary or special trains, as required by the Postmaster General.

These special mail trains eventually became Travelling Post Offices, aboard which mail was sorted by hand. Mail was first sorted on a moving train in January 1838, in a converted horsebox on the Grand Junction Railway, General Post Office surveyor Frederick Karstadt having come up with the idea.

The first special postal train was operated by the Great Western Railway between London and Bristol, on 1 February 1855, leaving Paddington at 8.46pm, and arriving at Bristol Temple Meads at 12.30am. In 1866, the first lineside apparatus for picking up and setting down mailbags without stopping was installed by the GWR, at Slough and Maidenhead.

The first railway stamp was issued in England in 1846 for the carriage of parcels by train, and under legislation of 1891, British railway companies were empowered to issue railway letter stamps for the conveyance of letters by rail. A few heritage lines like the Ffestiniog, Bluebell and Talyllyn railways carry on that tradition today.

Yet to take the mail by rail concept one stage further, what about a railway that was purposely designed for the exclusive carriage of mail?

One of the less-conspicuous exhibits in the Great Hall of the National Railway Museum in York is a train from London's famous Post Office underground railway.

This hidden 2ft gauge line, which ran in tunnels 70ft below the city's streets, ran for 19 hours a day, 286 days a year, on 23 miles of track. It had no drivers or guards, and was fully automated, controlled in its latter years by computer.

At one stage it was carrying more than four million items of post a day, and managed to

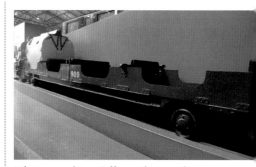

The preserved Post Office underground railway train inside the Great Hall at the National Railway Museum, where it sits alongside classic locomotives of the steam age.

Mount Pleasant Post Office tube station in operation in 1996.

This Pneumatic Dispatch Company atmospheric railcar designed for use in a 4ft tunnel dates from 1860 and is also now owned by the National Railway Museum. The concept of the pneumatic railway was the brainchild of British inventor George Medhurst in 1810, only a few years after Trevithick demonstrated his steam locomotives. Medhurst's idea was based around a carriage in an iron tube being blown along rails by compressed air.

run over its 6½-mile main line from Paddington at one end to Whitechapel at the other in 26 minutes.

It may have had no passengers, but it nonetheless had nine stations, the busiest being Mount Pleasant, which served two British Rail main line stations and major London sorting offices.

The concept of an underground railway just to carry mail dates back to 1853 when a 225-yard vacuum-operated tube began carrying letters and came to the attention of the Post Office.

In 1859, the Pneumatic Dispatch Company built a test line at Battersea, followed by a tube from its headquarters next to the Post Office's North Western District Office to the parcel office at Euston station. It was followed by a second line which was built from Euston to the General Post Office. It was not a financial success, and closed in 1874.

London's trademark traffic congestion had emerged as a major problem by early Edwardian times, when the motor car was still in its infancy and buses and vans were still pulled by horses. The GPO remembered the short-lived pneumatic line, and in 1908 despatched a team of engineers to inspect the Chicago Freight subway system and a similar system in Berlin, Germany.

Building of a subway system began in Chicago in 1899, and within seven years there was a tunnel under almost every downtown street. The 6ft wide and 7½ft high tunnels were meant to accommodate only telephone cables, but the Illinois Tunnel Company also secretly installed 2ft gauge railway tracks.

In 1911, the GPO produced plans for a tunnel railway from Whitechapel to Paddington to carry mail, and contractor John Mowlem & Co began tunnelling through the London clay in February 1915.

The work was suspended in 1917 due to the wartime shortage of labour and materials, and in the meantime the tunnels were used to house artworks from the Tate Gallery, National Portrait Gallery, British Museum and the Wallace Collection.

The scheme did not resume until 1925, and was again impeded the following year.

The first section, between Paddington and West Central District Office, was available for training in February 1927, and a year later, the first letter post was carried.

While the main railway tunnel is 70ft below ground, the stations were built at a much shallower depth, giving a 1-in-20 gradient into and out of each of them, so that the mail had less distance to travel from the platforms to the surface, and to aid deceleration of the trains on their approach to the stations, and help acceleration away.

The trains were powered by a 440V DC power centre rail and could run up to 40 mph.

Kilmarnock Engineering provided 90 4wRE (the suffix 'RE' means, third rail-powered electric locomotive) four-wheeled units with English Electric traction equipment for use on

POST OFFICE UNDERGROUND MAIL TRAIN: LONDON

A 1950s GPO poster by Lili Rethi entitled Post Office Underground Mail Train: London, *showing workers unloading mail trains.*

A Mail Rail train next to a deserted platform – uncanny for London's underground!

the railway, in sets of three. However, they were found to be difficult and costly to operate, because their 7ft 3in wheelbase was unsuitable for the very tight curves which caused repeated derailments.

In 1929, after trials with an articulated car and a bogie car, English Electric supplied 50 bogie 2w-2-2-2wRE type units, and after early problems with them were solved, another 10 were ordered in 1936.

During World War Two, the line was used as dormitories for GPO staff.

In 1954, because of problems of access at the Western District Office, Wimpole Street and the Western Central District Office, New Oxford Street, it was decided to build a new Western District Office at Rathbone Place, diverting the railway to run through its basement. Trains began running there in 1958, but it was not until 1965 that Postmaster General

Anthony Wedgwood-Benn officially opened the new office.

In 1962, two new prototype units were supplied by English Electric. Replacing the earlier stock, 34 units were supplied by Greenbat and Hunslet between 1980-82.

In 1993, a £750,000 computer began controlling the system from a central point.

By 2003, just three stations remained in use because the sorting offices above the others had been relocated. That year, Royal Mail announced that the underground railway was to be closed because it was five times as expensive to send parcels and letters along it than to use alternative road transport, despite road congestion.

The Communication Workers Union claimed the actual figure was closer to three times more expensive and argued in vain that the railway was being used at only one-third of its capacity. The Greater London Authority produced a report in support of Mail Rail, as the line had been known since its 60th anniversary, but nonetheless its last train ran on 31 May 2003.

Alternative uses for the line were considered. At one stage it was suggested that despite its claustrophobic nature, it might even become a tourist attraction, but that idea was quickly dismissed as the costs were too high.

People had, however, taken the story of the little train with no passengers than nobody ever saw to their hearts. Many of the trains found new homes like the Buckinghamshire Railway Centre, Amberley Museum in Sussex and the Launceston Steam Railway, where owner Nigel Bowman drew up an ingenious plan to build a narrow-gauge diesel multiple unit using adapted bogies from the Mail Rail trains. One such bogie was demonstrated at the Ffestiniog Railway's Quirks & Curiosities gala in May 2010.

Nigel Bowman and his wife Kay from the Launceston Steam Railway demonstrating their prototype railcar bogie, constructed with motors and wheelsets from Post Office Railway stock.

CHAPTER FOURTEEN
BAKER STREET TO BRILL: FAR FROM THE MADDING CROWD

THE WORDS 'LONDON UNDERGROUND' today immediately conjure up images of packed escalators leading to even more crowded platforms where commuters wait to be packed sardine-style into tube trains, for the rewards of reaching their intended destination in the national capital far quicker than if they tried to use surface transport. Welcome to the heart of the metropolis!

Despite the notorious peak-period discomfort, London has a transport system that is far better than those in many other cities around world, ferrying millions of people to and from work and the shops.

However, not all of the London Transport system was like this. Briefly contained within its vast portfolio of routes was a remote six-and-a-half mile branch serving a rural backwater that barely served a handful of passengers, and used steam traction which even in its day had the words 'museum exhibit' oozing from every orifice.

In deepest Buckinghamshire, 51 miles from the Baker Street terminus of the Metropolitan Line by train, and past the outer fringes of the fabled sprawling suburbia immortalised by Sir John Betjeman as Metroland, lay the village of Brill. In the mid-1930s, Brill was the furthest point that you could travel from the capital via London Underground, but few ever did.

These was no sign of the great labyrinthine network of electric trains which had followed in the wake of Magnus Volk's pioneering Brighton experiments.

Instead, ancient Metropolitan Railway steam locomotives hauled ageing wooden carriages back and forth from the junction with the main line at Quainton Road, a route into the heart of London jointly shared by the Met and the Great Central Railway. Before the Met old-timers were introduced, the Brill branch had used flywheel-driven geared locomotives more resembling road traction engines than traditional railway stock.

This eccentric little railway was built between 1870 and 1872 by the third Duke of Buckingham and Marquess of Chandos, who lived at the 18th-century Wotton House, and who served as chairman of the London & North Western Railway from 1853-61.

He wanted it for agricultural and industrial use on his estate, but it was also opened as a public railway. It was first known at the Wotton Tramway but later became the Brill Tramway.

Maybe a bit like Rocket, *but hardly rocket science: one of the Aveling & Porter chain-driven locomotives supplied to the Wotton Tramway in 1872, and now preserved by London Transport Museum.*

An early picture of one of the Aveling & Porter locomotives.

Above left: An Aveling & Porter engine hauling a passenger train on the Brill Tramway around 1890.

Above right: The Wotton Tramway was recreated at the Buckinghamshire Railway Centre when visiting 1895-built Aveling & Porter flywheel-driven locomotive Blue Circle, *which is broadly similar to the line's first two engines, hauled the venue's replica Brill Tramway coach.*

Metropolitan Railway A class locomotive No 23 of 1866 at the level crossing at Wood Siding station on the Brill branch, on 21 September 1934, after the line became part of the London Transport portfolio.

The initial section from Quainton Road to Wotton was brought into use on 1 April 1871, and the whole line to Brill, 700ft above sea level, was ready by summer 1872.

Running from Quainton Road (opened by the Aylesbury & Buckingham Railway in 1868), there were intermediate stations at Waddesdon (renamed Waddesdon Road in 1922 to distinguish it from Waddesdon Manor on the main line between Aylesbury and Quainton Road), Westcott, Wotton, Church Siding and Wood Siding.

Signalling was extremely basic with only one engine in use on the tramway at any one time. The tramway was initially operated by horses, but after a few months introduced its own locomotives which ran until 1906.

The first pair were 10-ton 0-4-0 single-cylinder geared steam locomotives supplied by Aveling & Porter, works numbers 807 and 846, and cost £400 each. Their maximum speed was about 8mph.

Both were later sold to Nether Heyford brickworks, near Weedon, Northamptonshire, which kept them until 1950. No 1 survives in the custody of London's Transport Museum.

The next two locomotives were supplied by WG Bagnall of Stoke-on-Trent, They comprised four-coupled saddle tank *Buckingham*, works number 16 of 1876, and 0-4-0 tank *Wootton*, No 120 of 1877. Both were unusual in having "reversed" inside cylinders to drive the front axle.

Schemes to extend the tramway from Brill to Oxford 10 miles away, were drawn up in 1883 and 1888, but both came to nothing.

The Oxford & Aylesbury Tramway Company took over the operation of the tramway in 1894 when the duke died. The company made many improvements to bring it up to date, replacing the original light rails laid on longitudinal sleepers with flat-bottomed rails spiked direct to transverse sleepers, and 'modernising' the rolling stock.

The Aveling & Porters were superseded by Manning Wardle industrial 0-6-0 saddle tanks with inside cylinders, one of them being replaced by another Manning Wardle in 1899. They were *Earl Temple*, works number 1249 of 1894, *Huddersfield*, works number 616, a secondhand locomotive built 1876, withdrawn 1899 and *Wotton No 2*, works number 1415, built 1899. *Earl Temple* was later renamed *Brill No 1*.

The Metropolitan Railway, which built the first physical link between the tramway and the main line, in December 1899 leased the tramway and introduced more new locomotives and rolling stock, but never exercised its option to buy the branch outright.

Betjeman visited Quainton Road in 1929 and later recalled watching the Brill branch train depart: "The steam ready to take two or three passengers through oil-lit halts and over level crossings, a rather bumpy journey."

In 1933 the London Passenger Transport Board was formed, taking over all the city's subterranean railway companies and unifying them into one body, creating the modern London Underground operation. Included in the job lot of lines inherited from the constituent companies was the Brill Tramway, which the powers that were certainly did not want.

With many rural light railways closing due to unbeatable competition from road transport, on 30 November 1935, the tramway's services were brought to an end.

Nothing remains of the tramway today, apart from privately-owned Westcott station. Passenger trains on the Great Central route from Marylebone to Nottingham ceased to call at Quainton Road from 1963, and on 3 September 1966, the complete route was closed to passengers apart from services between Nottingham and Rugby which lingered on until 1969.

Meanwhile, the London Railway Preservation Society which had been formed to save locomotives and stock from the steam age before they all disappeared acquired the use of Quainton Road station's goods yard as a base. Reforming as the Quainton Railway Society, it established what became the Buckinghamshire Railway Centre.

In the years that followed, two Aveling & Porter locomotives similar to those used on the tramway have been based at the centre at various times, and members even built a replica Brill Tramway coach to offer the public rides behind one of them.

In the early 21st century, the relaying of a mile of the tramway from Quainton Road westwards was mooted, but was finally quashed in 2010, when the Government announced the preferred route of its proposed London-Birmingham high speed rail route. The line will pass close to the centre and bisect the old tramway formation, leaving no way through.

AYLESBURY & BUCKINGHAM RAILWAY,
AND
WOTTON TRAMWAY.

Arrangements have been made by which **GOODS** and **PARCELS** can be Booked through, between AYLESBURY and the undermentioned Places in WOTTON TRAMWAY District, on and after 1st December next, (including collection or delivery,) at the following Rates, viz.:—

Ale and Porter	6d. per Cwt.
Groceries, in Mixed Packages	6d.
Hardware	6d.
Haberdashery and General Drapery	7½d.
Earthenware, in Casks and Crates	6d.
Leather	6d.
Iron and General Ironmongery	6d.
Wines and Spirits, in Casks and Cases	6d.
Ditto, in Hampers	7½d.
Ditto, in Jars or Bottles *(protected by basketwork)* 7½d.	
Ditto, *(protected by basketwork)* if in over 4-gall. size 9d.	
Single Parcels or Packages .. 6d. each.	Above 14lbs. and until more by weight 8d. each.

DELIVERIES MADE AS FOLLOWS:

Brill and Wotton	*Daily.*
Boarstall, Oakley, & Little London	*Wednesdays & Saturdays.*
Ham Green, Kingswood, Grendon, and Edgcott	*Tuesdays, Wednesdays, Fridays, and Saturdays.*
Dorton, Ashendon, and Pollicott	*Wednesdays & Saturdays.*
Ludgershall and Piddington	*Mondays and Thursdays.*

☞ Any further particulars can be obtained at the Offices of the Aylesbury and Buckingham Railway, Aylesbury; or any of the Offices on the Wotton Tramway.

Aylesbury, 12th November, 1872.

Printed 1870s freight tariff for the Wotton Tramway, with prices for the carriage of various types of material, delivery days and train times and other conditions.

As far from the madding crowd as you could get by London Transport: lonely Brill station as pictured in 1935.

CHAPTER FIFTEEN

MANX INSECT LIFE

Double header in 19in gauge: Bee, with Ant *behind, hauling three replica ore wagons.*

A WIDESPREAD APPLICATION – though largely unseen by the general public – of railways has been their use inside mines. Narrow gauge lines with locomotives vastly reduced in height, and in most cases battery-electric because steam with sparks and smoke would be totally unsuitable in a confined space.

One mine railway that did use steam locomotives was a curious 19in gauge tramway that served the Great Laxey Mine on the Isle of Man. This mine, once of the most successful lead and zinc mines in Britain, is a landmark feature of the island, courtesy of the great red 72ft 6ins diameter wheel, the *Lady Isabella*, built in 1864 to pump out water and keep the passages dry.

The mine's main level was the 1½-mile Adit Level and, entering the hillside beneath the wheel, was nearly one-and-a-half miles long.

A narrow-gauge tramway ran along the entire length of the Adit Level and took the extracted ore out of the mine to the washing floors where it was prepared for sale.

At first, the wagons were hauled by ponies, but in 1877 two tiny steam engines replaced them. They were constructed by Stephen Lewin & Company of Poole in Dorset, a firm far better known for building steamboats.

Ant and Bee *on passenger duties at Valley Gardens.*

Standing just 4ft 9in tall and 3ft wide, the pair, named *Ant* and *Bee*, could pull up to seven of the mine's 200 wagons each. They were too small to have cabs, and because of the low clearances in the tunnels, drivers had to remain seated.

The pair gave sterling service until the mine, which in 1875, had produced more than half the British output of zinc, closed. They were scrapped a few years later.

The island was and is famous for its antiquated railways and electric tramways. The Isle of Man Steam Railway which runs from Douglas to Port Erin is the remnant of a much larger network that had lines running from Douglas to Peel, Ramsey and Foxdale. The electric lines, the Manx Electric Tramway from Douglas to Laxey and Ramsey and the Snaefell Mountain Railway, survive in their entirety, while a 2ft gauge pleasure line, the Groudle Glen Railway, has been revived.

In a book on bizarre railways, it may also be appropriate to mention the Douglas Bay Horse Tramway which runs along a 3ft gauge track from the steam railway station for a mile along the island capital's promenade. Horse traction was the standard form of traction on railways before steam placed its foot in the door, but where else in Britain can you see it today on regular public transport services, run by the local authority, in this case Douglas Borough Council? The line survived both plans for electrification in 1908 and competition from buses.

With so many heritage railways on a comparatively small island, it came as a surprise when a new group, the Laxey and Lonan Heritage Trust, spearheaded by Richard Booth and Captain Stephen Carter, announced in 1999 that it intended to tackle the old mine line, setting a target date of 2004 to have it running again to mark the 150th anniversary of the *Lady Isabella*, which was named after the island governor's wife.

Much of the funding came from the estate of island resident Lt Col Randolph Glen.

A major stumbling block was removed in 1999 when a Manx Electric Railway housed in

Great Laxey Mine station at Valley Gardens with restored Snaefell Mine waterwheel in the background.

Ant returning to the mine workings with empty ore wagons, in a pre-World War One view.

Wasp, the line's battery-electric locomotive.

Bee *being prepared for its next journey.*

Lady Isabella, one of the trademarks of the Isle of Man, is the largest working waterwheel in the world and is the island's most visited tourist attraction.

the mine railways' 100ft tunnel at Laxey – the longest on the island – was relocated.

The revivalists could have easily opted for horse transport, but decided to go the whole hog, and ordered a fully-working full-size replica of *Ant* from miniature steam locomotive builder Great Northern Steam Ltd of Darlington, for £30,000.

As with the Steam Elephant, no original drawings for the pair survived, and a new set had to be compiled, from drawings for replacement boilers, safety valves and regulators supplied by Stafford firm WG Bagnall in 1905, some dimensions given in a 1902 edition of *The Locomotive Magazine* and contemporary photographs.

The trust by this stage were bitten by the steam bug, and while Ant was under construction, they ordered a replica of *Bee* into the bargain. Two tiny 'manrider' carriages were built by modern-day rolling stock manufacturer and restorer Alan Keef Ltd of Ross-on-Wye, so that passengers can now ride along the line where loaded wagons of ore were once hauled from the mine.

The restored railway was officially opened on 25 September 2004.

In 2006, the Laxey Mines Research Group, in conjunction with the heritage trust, completed the restoration of the 50ft 6ins diameter former Snaefell Mine waterwheel at the line's Valley Gardens terminus. It looks like a little sister of the *Lady Isabella*.

A refurbished Clayton battery locomotive was obtained from Alan Keef in 2009, and staying with the insect theme, was given the name *Wasp*. The railway also has six replica ore wagons which were made by the Laxey blacksmith. The railway is also unusual both in running beneath at one point, the abovementioned tunnel, another heritage line, the Manx Electric Railway, and having replicas of its entire original fleet.

CHAPTER SIXTEEN
A FAIRYTALE CASTLE'S DEEPEST SECRET

TO THE GREAT WESTERN Railway publicity department, the fairytale Cornish island of St Michael's Mount was a godsend.

To anyone designing posters or brochures enticing holidaymakers to travel to the westernmost outpost of the Paddington empire, the wooded rocky outcrop topped by its romantic castle, had a decidedly 'wow' factor.

As the GWR main line runs south from St Erth on the last leg of its journey to Penzance, the island suddenly appears as a 'must see' jewel in a glistening blue sea fringed by palm trees.

At one stage you could stop off at Marazion which is connected to the island with its miniature harbour and fishing village at low tide by a granite causeway, but the station was closed to passengers on 5 October 1964, with freight services following on 6 December 1965. For years several Pullman coaches which had been converted into holiday lets were sited there, but the last was removed in 2006 and the station building has been restored as a private house.

Guidebooks will tell you that St Michael's Mount was Ictis, the place where the great seafarers of the ancient world, the Phoenicians, traded in tin from Cornish mines long before the Romans came.

It also features heavily in the legends of the lost land of Lyonesse, which stretched from Land's End to the Isles of Scilly and which was engulfed in a single night by a tsunami caused by Merlin the magician in revenge for the death of King Arthur.

Boatman Dave Ladner unloads the train at the harbour station.

The low-tide causeway running from Marazion to the fairytale island of St Michael's Mount.

The island's Cornish name means 'hoar rock in the wood', indicating that it once lay several miles from the coast and was surrounded by trees: indeed, the stumps of a prehistoric forest can sometimes be seen at very low tides.

Other tales have linked it with the archangel Michael and a giant called Cormoran who later perished at the hands of Jack the Giant Killer.

The castle dates back to the activities of a group of 11th century Benedictine monks from the very similar Mont St Michel in Normandy who built a priory on the summit. As a result, long before the GWR publicity machine went into overdrive about the far west, St Michael's Mount attracted tourists in the form of pilgrims to the priory, which survived until Henry VIII dissolved the monasteries. The remains of the priory were subsequently rebuilt into a castle.

However, what none of the guidebooks, including those published by the GWR, will tell you, is that like all great fairytale castles, it has a dark secret of its own. A railway one for that matter.

Top: *This giant buffer stop at the bottom station ensures that the train never comes into contact with unsuspecting passers-by on the harbour side.*

Above: *The entrance from the quayside to the 'tramyard.' The short length of 2ft 5in gauge rail set in the quayside is the only part of the railway that the public get to see.*

Right: *The romantic castle served by the underground railway.*

For beneath the Mount runs a railway, linking the castle at the top to the harbour at the bottom, and very few of the 200,000 annual visitors to the island, since 1954 in the care of the National Trust, ever notice it.

The railway, which is around an eighth of a mile long, is not a model, or a rich owner's plaything, but a real working freight-carrying operation, one that has successfully operated almost every day since it was built in 1901 to replace the packhorses which previously hauled supplies up the steep Mount.

It is a unique 2ft 5in gauge cable-operated incline line. Once operated at speeds of up to 40mph, it boasts a slope of 1-in-1.9 as it climbs 174ft from the bottom to the summit.

The bottom station lies next to the island's quayside, from where supplies for the castle are loaded into a wagon. Its top station is a room in the castle's kitchen pantry – and the run between the two is non stop!

The only public clue to the existence of the railway is the short length of rail laid tramway-style on the quayside beyond a set of wooden double doors between the harbourside cottages that lead to its base station, known as the 'tramyard' and nowadays contained in a steel cage for security.

The tunnel inside the granite Mount.

Apart from one section where tunnelling was unavoidable, the line was built by Cornish miners using a 'cut and cover' method with a brick archway, to conceal the railway from view.

The miners' practice of spiking the rails directly on to the rock face was used for much of its length. Some of the original rails were still in place and in regular use a century later.

The line has never seen a steam engine, or a locomotive of any description for that matter. It has but a single item of rolling stock, a wagon which is hauled up and down the line by a cable connected to an electric-operated winding drum at the summit.

Alongside the 'tramyard' stands the engine house, which contains the old winding machinery which became redundant when health and safety regulations forced the line's 'modernisation' in 1988. As originally designed, the winding gear was at the bottom. The power for the winding mechanism was originally supplied by a gas engine, but a Ruston petrol engine replaced it in the 1920s. When an 11,000-volt power cable supplying the island from the mainland was laid in 1951, this engine was in turn replaced by a Crompton Parkinson motor.

Inside the engine house, a system was operated whereby white marks had to line up on each of three giant cog wheels on the winding gear in the base station to indicate that the brake should be applied; if a miscalculation was made or there was a lack of concentration, gravity would take its course and the wagon would end up wherever the maximum slack allowed.

Prior to the 1988 upgrading, there had been several accidents on the railway, some of which led to the wagon overshooting the buffer stops, smashing through the quayside wall ...

The winding gear at the top.

65

Waiting for the train at the summit station.

and ending up in the briny.

From the harbour station, where the wagon is unloaded and loaded, the line passes from daylight into the tunnel which is 5ft wide and 7ft tall and starts its ascent to the summit on a slight curve.

The tunnel begins on a slope of 1-in-14, increasing to 1-in-4 over the first 250ft, and is lit by electric lamps at regular intervals.

An upturn after this first stage takes the line up a 1-in-3 gradient for a distance of 160ft before reaching a 120ft section on a level of 1-in-1.9.

Nearing the summit, the roof height diminishes to 6ft where the tunnel runs through the granite.

The journey originally ended next to the top station, known as the 'coal station'. It was situated alongside the boiler house just below the kitchens. The boiler provides heating for the castle, but coal is no longer carried by the railway as the boiler is now oil fired. However, the oil is piped through the tunnel.

At the 'coal station', supplies were unloaded with the wagon held by the cable in near-vertical position on the 1-in-1.9 gradient. Goods were often unloaded by a winch fixed to the adjacent wall of the castle, hoisted over an adjacent roof and lowered through holes in the ceilings of two storerooms serving the castle kitchens, which are out of bounds to the public.

The 1988 modifications included the building of a 20ft extension above the 'coal station', to what once served as a pantry for the kitchen. The summit station, now referred to as the 'pantry', allows the wagon to be unloaded almost on the level.

The train takes around 2mins 35secs to complete its journey.

Before World War Two, serious consideration was given to converting the line for passenger use, but no action was taken. Staff who worked there have tales of riding inside the wagon as a clandestine dare, even though it was strictly against the rules.

St Michael's Mount is a prime example of one of the most extreme uses of the railway concept in the British Isles, but one of the most effective. British Railways never had it in its empire, and it never came to the attention of Dr Beeching, and so it is still running today, although public access is not permitted.

What's more, the railway is one legend about St Michael's Mount that is incontrovertibly true!

CHAPTER SEVENTEEN

BROADCASTS FROM BRISTOL'S FORGOTTEN UNDERGROUND

THE USE OF ROPE or cable-worked railways on steep inclines is in itself not usual, nor is it, like the self-propelled locomotive, a British invention.

The world's oldest funicular railway – a name derived from the Latin funiculus, or funis, meaning 'rope' – is the Reisszug, a private line which supplied freight to Hohensalzburg Castle at Salzburg in Austria and is mentioned in records from 1515. Originally using wooden rails and a hemp haulage rope, it was operated by human or animal power. It is still operational today, but employs steel rails, steel cables and an electric motor on the same route through the castle's fortifications.

Canals used inclined planes to tackle steep hills in a relatively-short space of time.

The concept of using rope to haul wagons up and down steep gradients which cannot be worked by horses has manifested itself in many different forms: inclined planes on canals as an alternative to lock staircases, inclined railways like County Durham's pioneering Stanhope & Tyne line which had several of them, and cliff railways, built to link 'upper' and 'lower' parts of seaside resorts, or in the case of Bridgnorth, inland towns.

A development of the rope-worked incline was the water-balance incline, where a wheeled water tank would be coupled to descending wagons on one of a pair of tracks, while a rope connected via a pulley would raise empty wagons on the other line. When the water carrier reached the bottom, it would be emptied, and the empty water carrier on the train that had reached the summit refilled. Many funicular railways placed the water tank beneath a passenger carriage.

Britain once had 35 passenger-carrying cliff railways, most of them constructed in Victorian times to serve the booming resorts that developed rapidly once they were linked to the national railway network.

The country's first was a water-balance operation opened at Scarborough in 1875, connecting clifftop spa buildings to South Bay below.

Two suburbs of Bristol, however, found themselves linked by the most bizarre variation on the theme – not only a cliff railway that was built underground (as was the Folkestone line) but had four tracks, (whereas Folkestone had two), but uniquely served both its city and

A hand-coloured postcard of the Clifton Rocks Railway in operation.

The surviving cable winding gear and the railway tracks at the top station in September 2009, with a mock-up of a car front below.

The removal of the passenger cars in 1941 to make way for wartime installations.

The white metal medallion issued to passengers on the line's first day of operation.

country long after the last trains ran and were cut up for scrap.

The Clifton Rocks Railway was a giant piece of social engineering, in linking the genteel middle-class suburb of Clifton, the 'cliff town' with downmarket Hotwells alongside the River Avon, a failed spa resort where the mineral waters, first recorded in 1480, were found to be polluted, and which was the haunt of drunken sailors.

Clifton residents wanted to remain aloof, both in social and topographical terms, and even fought against the introduction of trams from Bristol city centre.

Two schemes to build a cliff railway linking the two disparate settlements were mooted in 1880 and 1889, but were unsuccessful. However, in 1890, publisher George Newnes, later MP for Newmarket, Cambridgeshire, produced plans for an inclined lift from Hotwells Road to the garden of No 14 Princes Buildings, which now includes the modern-day Avon Gorge Hotel. His scheme countered the opposition to the previous schemes in that it would not disfigure the cliff faces of the limestone Avon Gorge but would run behind them in a tunnel.

Newnes had been largely responsible for financing the water-powered Lynton & Lynmouth Cliff Railway, designed by George Croydon Marks, later Baron Marks of Woolwich, and which opened on Easter Monday 1890, and is still with us today.

He was also heavily involved with the building of the Lynton & Barnstaple Railway.

Newnes' scheme for the Avon Gorge was approved by Bristol's Merchant Venturers on condition he resurrected Clifton as a spa resort with the building of a hydropathic institute next door to the top station, the Royal Clifton Spa having been demolished in 1867. Newnes readily agreed and building started on 7 March 1891 when Lady Wathen, wife of Lord Mayor Sir Charles Wathen, fired the first shot to start the tunnel excavation.

The lower terminus was on Hotwells Road, near the Bristol Port & Pier Railway's Hotwells station, and the upper in Sion Hill. The luxury of four tracks mirrored the high expectations for traffic. Each line was 450ft long over a 1-in-2.1 gradient and built to 3ft 2in gauge, with a fleet of four 18-seater cars.

The cars were operated as connected pairs using the water-balance method. The water emptied from the cars into a reservoir at the lower station was pumped back to one at the upper level by four-stroke gas engines. A cabin at the upper station housed the railway controller who was equipped with a handbrake for the cable pulley sheaves. The tunnel was lit by gas.

The official opening took pace on 11 March 1893, with 6220 passengers making return trip. The journey took 40 seconds and passengers were charged a penny to go up and four pence to go back down. On the opening day, each passenger was given a commemorative gilded white metal medallion in the shape of a Maltese cross with a picture of the cars on one side together with the initials of the promoter, engineer and architect.

It was an instant hit, with 427,492 passengers carried in the first year, but this turned out to be a best-ever, with numbers steadily declining afterwards.

The Clifton Spa Pump Room was opened in 1894, drawing spa water from Hotwells via a 350ft borehole, and it was followed four years later by the Clifton Grand Spa Hydro.

On 29 September 1912 the railway was sold for £1500 to the Bristol Tramways & Carriage Co Ltd, after going bankrupt. The new owner tried offering a threepenny 'round robin' ticket involving a return trip from Bristol by tram, funicular and bus, but another major blow came in 1922 when the Bristol Port & Pier Railway which served Hotwells closed. Bus competition finally killed off the funicular which last ran on 29 September 1934.

The railway was left to sleep, only to be awakened in 1940. The forgotten railway was taken over by three organisations as part of the war effort.

Imperial Airways constructed an office suite there and used the upper section of the tunnel for storage and for repairing barrage balloons. It took over the Pump Room, which had

BBC broadcasters at work during World War Two.

Left: The bottom station at Hotwells, with an electric tram running along side the River Avon and the suspension bridge in the background.

An early 20th-century view of the top station in Sion Hill.

69

Above left: *The surviving turnstiles inside the top station.*

Above right: *An original lamp from the top station found in the debris inside the tunnel has been reinstalled to its rightful place: the bracket was stolen by a student as a prank in the 1960s but he returned it when he saw that restoration was being attempted.*

previously been used as a ballroom and a cinema, and used it as its administrative headquarters.

In the middle of the tunnel, three air raid shelters were built by the Ministry of Works. It became public shelter No 1898, and hundreds of people crowded inside when sirens sounded.

At the bottom of the line, the BBC established its wartime emergency communication headquarters outside London. While it was, thankfully, never needed as such, the site become a key part of the national transmitting network, relaying broadcasts from London to West of England transmitters.

It was certainly a new and unexpected lease of life for the funicular, which was water-proofed, had electric lighting installed and was divided into seven chambers including a BBC studio, control room and transmitters. Sadly, the four cars were dismantled to make way for the alterations and scrapped.

After the war, the BBC kept its transmitter operational as a local booster station until 24 March 1960, but now it is used only for telephone cables.

The Pump Room, last used as a ballroom in the 1970s, and the tunnel are now owned by the Avon Gorge Hotel. Since 2005, a volunteer charity, The Friends of the Clifton Rocks Railway, has preserved as many of the tunnel artefacts as possible, showcasing them in a small museum at the upper station which is opened to the public on special occasions, and dreams of achieving the full restoration of the line. Such a project would cost up to £15-million at 2010 prices, and feasibility studies are being planned.

It is unlikely that it would serve a public transport use, as there is nothing to attract visitors to Hotwells, but as a heritage attraction with a multitude of stories to tell, it might well sit alongside Brunel's nearby suspension bridge and SS *Great Britain* as another jewel in Bristol's proud crown.

Funicular lines in Britain are by no means limited to carrying passengers. The Lizard lifeboat station in Cornwall is accessed by one, while a private cliff railway was built at Sennen near Land's End to take goods up and down from a house – staking a claim for Britain's westernmost mainland railway!

CHAPTER EIGHTEEN
THE CAR IS KING

RICHARD TREVITHICK turned to building railway locomotives after he found that his pioneering self-propelled road vehicles could not be supported by the muddy pot-holed highways of his day. Had they been able to do so, transport technology would almost certainly have taken a different direction.

The railway remained the principal form of transport in Britain until the 1950s. By then, levels of car ownership had risen to the point where many branch lines become uneconomical to run and were closed years before anyone had heard of Dr Beeching.

The flooding of the secondhand market by surplus army lorries after World War One paved the way for entrepreneurs to launch their own haulage businesses and compete directly with railways for freight traffic.

Road vehicles offer infinitely greater flexibility than railways, especially as far as the individual owner or operator is concerned, whereas trains have to stay on one track. Once they were affordable to the public at large, and the roads were good enough to carry them, the advantage of railways exploited by Trevithick was largely lost.

Adrian Shooter's Model T Ford at Rhiw Goch farm crossing on the Ffestiniog Railway in May 2010.

The rail-adapted Model T Ford on the private Statfold Barn Railway near Tamworth.

The Sandy River & Rangeley Lakes Railroad's Ford Model T inspection saloon of 1925.

However, not all road vehicles aimed to compete with the railways. A few wanted to run on them!

Over the May Day Bank holiday weekend in 2010, the Ffestiniog Railway held a 'Quirks and Curiosities' gala in which weird and wonderful forms of traction and rolling stock were displayed on the line.

One of the star exhibits was a Ford Model T, with its rubber tyres replaced by flanged wheels so it could run on 2ft gauge.

The original 1927-built car had been restored and transformed into a self-powered locomotive which requires no steering.

It has an engine powerful enough to reach speeds up to 60mph, but unlike more conventional railway rolling stock, it can only seat four passengers.

Owned by Chiltern Railways supremo Adrian Shooter, who has his own private 2ft gauge line, the Beeches Light Railway, at his Oxfordshire home, and who commissioned the conversion, it follows a historical precedent.

In 1925, a Model T – introduced in 1908 and held to be the world's first affordable automobile, the car which "put America on wheels", and of which more than 15 million were made – was similarly converted into a track inspection car for the 2ft gauge Sandy River & Rangeley Lakes Railroad in Maine. The vehicle still survives.

The Hunslet Engine Company team which converted Adrian's car worked from photographs of the prototype and some simple general arrangement drawings. The underframe incorporates a turntable device so the car can be turned at the end of a branch line – giving it a decided advantage over a conventional steam engine!

Adrian's model raised many eyebrows when it visited the 2ft gauge Launceston Steam Railway in Cornwall at Christmas 2009, after going there to have modified brakes fitted, and ending up running on the line.

Also in 1925, the New Zealand Railways Department, as part of its experiments with railcars, used Model T chassis and other equipment as the basis for two lightweight RM class Model T Ford railcars, but the experiment was not a success. Following problems with rough riding and overheating, they were withdrawn in 1931. One of the bodies survive, but is unrestored. Other countries similarly adapted Model T chassis to rail, but no other examples survive.

However, two replicas have been built, one in the USA and one to the New Zealand design by the country's Pleasant Point Museum and Railway, where it regularly runs.

Road-rail vehicles appear to offer the best of both worlds. A railcar of this type would be able to run along a rural branch line and take to the road at the terminus, accessing sparsely-populated areas where it would never be economically justifiable to build a railway.

However, only one of the 'Big Four' railway companies gave serious attention to the concept as far as the conveyance of passengers was concerned..

In 1932, the London, Midland & Scottish Railway trialled Huddersfield manufacturer Karrier's Ro-Railer, a hybrid 26-seater single-decker bus capable of running on both road and rail. It took five minutes to adapt the wheels from rail to road and vice versa.

The vehicle was tested on the 'Nicky Line' which linked Hemel Hempstead and Harpenden to Redbourn, and also on the Stratford-upon-Avon & Midland Junction Railway. The LMS approached Karrier after buying a mansion on the outskirts of Stratford and converting it into the Welcombe Hotel.

The Ro-Railer collected passengers at the hotel, took them to the station and ran on the tracks from Stratford to Blisworth, Northamptonshire, linking to a London service.

It lasted only two months in service before the LMS ditched the experiment and returned the vehicle to Karrier. Patronage was disappointing and it was said to have been too heavy for its chassis.

During World War Two, the chassis was converted for use as a conventional lorry while the body was sold off for use as a holiday home.

Karrier later supplied the London & North Eastern Railway with a road lorry tractor unit

The experimental Karrier Ro-Railer single-decker bus in LMS livery approaches Stratford Old Town station during its brief trial on the Stratford-upon-Avon & Midland Junction Railway in 1932.

A road-rail Ford Ranger on Australia's 2ft 6in gauge Puffing Billy Railway.

Graham Lee's rail-mounted Series IIa long-wheelbase Land Rover at the Statfold Barn Railway. It was built in 1969 as a hard top and in recent times converted to truck cab and to operate on 2ft gauge by the construction of two bogies. The transmission is driven from the original back axle now located higher in the chassis, driving the rear bogie via a series of chains.

mounted on flanged wheels with buffers fitted at both the front and rear. It was used for track maintenance on the West Highland line. Since then, rail-mounted road vehicles for permanent way duties have been produced by various manufacturers around the world.

Deutsche Bundesbahn operated special buses known as the Schi-Stra-Bus in Koblenz from the 1950s to 1970s. They were capable of being fitted with separate bogies.

The New South Wales Railways experimented with road-rail vehicles during the 1970s, while Canadian company Brandt has adapted large lorry tractor units for use as locomotives that can move by road to where they are needed. They can be used to haul normal service trains on smaller lines, or rescue larger trains that have broken down.

Adrian's adapted Model T is not unique today. In recent years, several vehicles have been similarly converted, often by enthusiasts, to run on rails.

The somewhat eccentric Spurn Head military railway not only had sail trolleys, as we saw earlier, but also ran a converted pre-World War One Itala racing car converted to rail operation by army officer Lieutenant Lees of the Royal Engineers. It was in use on the standard gauge line from at least February 1918 and remained in service until at least 1940, repeatedly modified in Heath Robinson style as and when original components wore out. It was said to be capable of 60mph.

A recent example is Hunslet Engine Company managing director Graham Lee's rail-mounted Land Rover, which runs on his 2ft gauge private Statford Barn Railway near Tamworth, Staffordshire.

The bus on rails concept did not die, but has reappeared at a handful of places around the world as guided bus systems, the first in Britain being the experimental Tracline 65 system which opened on West Midlands Travel's route 65 serving east Birmingham in 1984 but lasted only a few years, even though it did boost passenger numbers.

However, instead of running on railway tracks, the bus has a concrete dedicated 'trackway' of its own, where it is guided purely by the kerbs, the driver not having to steer as is the case with trains, and can reach much higher speeds free of traffic congestion. The guided buses, which have small guide wheels attached for engaging vertical kerbs on either side of the trackway, can also run on normal roads.

The concept, a sort of Haytor Tramway meets Ro-Railer, has been slow to take off, and is used in only a handful of cities around the world. Local people were therefore surprised when it was decided to convert the mothballed former Great Eastern Railway St Ives–Cambridge line into a two-track guided busway to ease the notorious congestion on the A14 trunk road between Huntingdon and the city.

A local pro-rail protest group, CAST.IRON (the Cambridge and St Ives Railway Organisation) campaigned against it on the basis that simply reviving the railway would cost a fraction of the busway's estimated £116-million cost, and that new Ro-Railer-type vehicles to run through the city centre would be built. A total of 2,735 objections were received from local councils, public bodies, transport interests, local pressure groups and individuals. Amongst the other objections was that it would become a monopoly because few bus operators could afford the expensive vehicles to run over it. Why go to the trouble of providing a pair of huge concrete tracks when it would be simpler to surface the railway trackbed to create a bus-only conventional road. Finally, the project would lack the versatility of rail because no incoming trains could run over it, or use vehicles from anywhere else.

A public inquiry was held in 2005, but the Labour government approved the scheme in December 2005. Construction began in March 2007 with an intended completion date of April 2009, But after delays, the busway finally opened on 7 August 2011. At 16 miles it is the longest operational guided busway in the world, overtaking the O-Bahn Busway in Adelaide. A deal whereby Stagecoach and Whippet Coaches would have exclusive use of the route for five years in exchange for providing a minimum service frequency daily between 7am and 7pm was signed with promoter Cambridgeshire County Council.

However, one local MP joined many locals in calling the scheme a "white elephant" and when I asked the question, one County Councillor privately admitted that the sole reason for choosing a guided busway was that the Government has asked for it and was footing much of the bill. At the time of writing, the question remains: will guided busways supersede railways and conventional road buses big time, or will the very expensive Cambridge scheme become another classic example of one of Britain's bizarre railways?

West Midlands Travel's brochure for its short-lived Tracline 65 guided bus system in Birmingham. The 600 yards of concrete experimental track required a line of mature trees to be felled, much to the anger of residents.

Initial trials on the Cambridgeshire guided busway.

CHAPTER NINETEEN

THREE ISLAND FORTRESSES

AS AN ISLAND NATION, the defence of our realm by sea has always been paramount. There are many examples of railways being built to construct or service fortifications that at various stages in our history been emplaced along the coast, as we saw earlier with the Spurn Head Railway.

In order to protect the mainland, some of these railways have been built on islands themselves, guarding the entrances to ports and harbours from enemy attack.

The Thames and Medway estuaries have over the centuries been a soft target as far as invasion threats from the Continent were concerned. The Vikings first struck Sheppey in 835, and continued into the 11th century. The rebel Earl Godwin raided Sheppey from Flanders in 1052, French and Spaniards attacked the north Kent coast in 1379, while 72 Dutch naval ships attacked and briefly occupied Sheerness in June 1667.

One big advantage in defending the Medway estuary is the plethora of small islets, mudflats and marshes which could be fortified.

In 1860, as fears arose about a potential war with Napoleon III's France (he was actually quite fond of the British), Lord Palmerston ordered a huge ring of fortifications to be built around the south coast of England and Wales. Circular forts built on Hoo Island and the smaller Darnet Island on the opposite side of the Medway channel were completed in 1871 and maintained until the early 20th century, and the buildings still survive.

Hoo, an uninhabited island a mile long and 700 yards wide under control of the Admiralty, has a short tramway to serve the fort, but around 1900 a 2ft 6in gauge steam railway system over three miles long was laid to transport materials for sea bank protection works. The gauge was chosen because it was identical to that of the navy's Chattenden & Upnor Railway on the mainland nearby.

The first locomotive, an Avonside 0-4-0 tank engine numbered 1 and named *Ascension*, was supplied by Avonside of Bristol, works number 1480 of 1904.

Bagnall supplied an 0-4-0 saddle tank, *Nipper*, No 1895 of 1909,

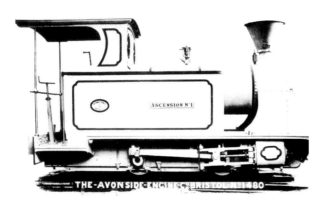

Works photograph of Avonside 0-4-0T Ascension No 1.

and *Ness*, No 1947 of 1912. A fourth steam engine, Kerr Stuart 0-4-0 tank No 749 of 1902 *Sirdar* is thought to have worked on Hoo Island during World War One.

Steam was abandoned around 1926 in favour of petrol-engined locomotives, of which four were acquired and operated there during World War Two.

The railway was converted to 2ft gauge in 1952, along with two of the locomotives. In 1961, two Hibberd diesels were delivered, Nos 3982 and 3983.

The island railway became disused in the seventies, its role of transporting dredged mud from the island wharf to tipping sites taken over by pipelines and tracked vehicles.

Responsibility for Hoo Island passed to the Department of the Environment after naval activities in the Medway were called down.

Because the island remains out of bounds, the Hoo Island system remains the most mysterious of Britain's island railways.

Two narrow gauge railways were laid to serve Palmerston forts on the opposite side of England, not during Victorian times but during World War Two.

The docks at Cardiff and Newport were a prime target for Luftwaffe bombers which flew over Weston-super-Mare and the Bristol Channel. In the middle of the Severn estuary, where it becomes open sea, are two distinctive islands, Flat Holm and Steep Holm, shaped exactly as their names suggest, and which geologically form the westernmost part of the limestone Mendip Hills.

They may seem from the shore to be mere lumps of grass-topped rock, although Flat Holm has a lighthouse. Yet their history dates back many centuries: it is believed that St Gildas wrote the first history of Britain on Steep Holm in the sixth century.

Hibberd diesels Nos 3983 and 3982 outside the Hoo Ness Island Railway's engine shed in 1983, long after the line had fallen into disuse.

Hoo Ness Island, as seen from the mainland.

Flat Holm had its own railway during World War Two.

Like Hoo Island, both had Palmerston forts built on them, and perhaps even more surprisingly, they also had operational railways – plural in the case of Steep Holm.

Following the evacuation from Dunkirk in 1940, Britain remained on 24-hour invasion alert. Fortifications were built at every conceivable 'weak' point across the country, and the islands' old Palmerston defences were revived 70 years on.

Lying beneath the flight path of bombers, these islands were the guardians of the shipping lane leading to the Port of Bristol and afforded protection to the Atlantic convoys which would rendezvous in the channel.

Track materials which had been held in store at the Longmoor Military Railway since World War One were brought to the islands. The components had previously been used in trench lines on the Western Front; David Benger, battery commander on Flat Holm from 1941-44, believed the rail, enough to lay near 45 miles of track at least, was of German origin and had been 'captured' in 1918.

On Flat Holm, where 350 soldiers were stationed to man batteries which had been superimposed on the Victorian defences when refortification started in spring 1941, 29 (Railway Survey) Company of the Royal Engineers found it to be fairly easy to lay a railway once the material had been brought from the tiny harbour to the top of the flat plateau. The 1ft 11½in gauge railway used diesel locomotives and wagons – also captured from the Germans – to convey ammunition, materials and provisions from a jetty at East Beach across

A Flat Holm gun battery in action against the Luftwaffe.

Steep Holm island, viewed from the enormous shingle spit which appears off East Beach, as the brown estuarine waters recede at low tide.

the island. The wagons were raised to the plateau by a short incline railway, leading to what was known as the railway 'terminus' from which lines spread out across the island summit.

An old cholera isolation hospital built to house infected sailors returning to Cardiff was turned into a NAAFI, a cinema and concert hall, while the island's farmhouse was used as the officers' mess.

After Flat Holm became non-operational in December 1944, German prisoners of war removed most of the equipment from the military occupation with comparative ease, lifting the railway the following year, and apart from one piece of rail soon nothing remained to remind anyone a railway had existed there.

Steep Holm was different. There, Indian Army soldiers with mule teams carried much of the equipment up the island's incline path, which follows a natural fault in the limestone strata, up to the summit.

Building supplies and military equipment were deposited on the shingle East Beach by tank landing craft prior to the construction of a 120ft-long girder landing-jetty by the Royal Engineers.

A railway was laid up the incline path in order to speed up the construction of the desperately-needed gun emplacements as the air raids intensified.

A fisherman's cottage and a pub which had served sailors on passing ships waiting to enter the port of Bristol were dynamited by 930 Port Construction and Repair Company to make way for the railway.

The cable-operated incline line was made up of rails fixed to metal sleepers, in three separate sections on the zig-zag incline path. At the top of each of the three sections was a set of points and a diesel-operated winch house. Trucks were loaded on the jetty using a diesel crane. They were coupled together to the front truck. The train was then hauled up the

Right: The railway track still in place on Steep Holm's incline path. The metal sleepers have been covered with soil to make it easier for the Kenneth Allsop Memorial Trust's Honda Power Carrier to take supplies to the restored barracks at the summit.

Far right: The separate incline line leading from the summit of Steep Holm to South Landing.

inclines by each winch in turn, reversing at the end of each zig-zag section.

The 1-in-2/3 gradient of the path caused problems for the trucks, which each had an 8cwt capacity. The profiles of the rails were bent with oxyacetylene torches to provide greater adhesion.

At the top of the incline, a diesel locomotive, possibly a Hunslet 0-4-0, hauled the wagons which carried vast quantities of sand and cement to the various construction sites and sidings around the 256ft summit. The wagons may also have either been pulled by mules or pushed by hand. The track may eventually have extended to two-thirds of a mile.

The line was used to help build a new set of four gun batteries, searchlight positions, generator houses and a battery observation post. Around 200 men were based on the island and housed in the refurbished Palmerston barracks.

After building work ended and track on the summit was largely lifted, the incline railway remained in use for bringing in fresh ammunition and general supplies.

A second incline railway was built in response to fears that bad weather would make the jetty unusable. An alternative landing point was constructed below the southern cliffs. South Landing, as it was called, was also served by a winch-operated railway linking it to the path which circuits the summit of the island.

Conditions on the island were harsh, with no natural supplies of water. There was an outbreak of typhoid fever which resulted in a ban on the eating of seagull eggs for fear of infection. Several men were injured falling over the sheer limestone cliffs in the blackout.

Unlike Flat Holm, the terrain of Steep Holm made it economically unviable, let alone impractical, to justify the removal of much of the military hardware after the war, including the incline railway. Just as the island's ten massive Victorian 7in muzzle-loading cannons were left in situ, so the little railway is still there for all to see today.

The line cannot be restored for safety reasons, as a runaway truck would almost certainly conflict with pedestrian usage of the sole path to the summit.

The Kenneth Allsop Memorial Trust, which has managed the island as a nature reserve in honour of the late broadcaster and naturalist since 1974, and has restored the barracks as a tea room, shop and museum, runs boat trips on selected days from Knightstone Harbour at Weston-super-Mare aboard the vessel *Bristol Queen*, so if you want to see this unique heritage railway before it finally rusts away in the salt sea air, you have the perfect chance.

One word of warning: the gulls are now firmly in charge of the 63-acre island, and they will never tire of letting you know.

The only known photograph of the East Beach landing jetty shows railway tracks with wagons.

CHAPTER TWENTY
WE DON'T LIKE TO BE BESIDE THE SEASIDE!

ON 16 JULY 2010, a new exhibition of seaside miniature railways opened in Cleethorpes. Located in two shop units opposite the town's 15in gauge Cleethorpes Coast Light Railway, it is intended to be the start of a national museum of miniature railways.

The location is certainly appropriate, for Lincolnshire has had its fair share of miniature lines at resorts like Skegness and Mablethorpe, where generations of children marvelled at the cut-down live steam versions of full-size prototypes and rode behind them. By the mid 20th-century, miniature seafront railways were part and parcel of the traditional British holiday, with every bucket and spade resort having at least one.

The county also boasted a seaside line at first exclusively patronised by youngsters, who were remodelling the coast on a slightly bigger scale than the average sandcastle. And unlike

Spoil being tipped to build up the sea wall at Freiston Shore, as seen in the early 1970s.

Serious sandcastling… but never for fun. These offenders are building sea defences by hand, just as navvies carved out cuttings and built embankments on railways in the 19th century. Would their misdemeanours have seen them let off with an ASBO today, I wonder?

most of the happy campers elsewhere on the coast, their stay lasted much longer than one or two weeks.

It was Britain's first, and only, prison railway.

In 1935, a group of 32 male young offenders were ordered to march all the way from Stafford to the bleakest part of the Lincolnshire coast 100 miles away, supervised by three warders and sleeping in village halls overnight. When they reached a patch of farmland where the River Witham meets The Wash east of Boston, they erected tents, which remained as their accommodation until they had constructed their own brick-built detention centre.

The aim of what was designed to be a new type of Borstal institution was to develop self-sufficiency, with the inmates running their own farm, but having to reclaim 600 acres of salt marsh in the process.

There was obviously a ready supply of free labour, but first they had to build a sea wall and drainage ditches to keep the waves back, a process that had been ongoing here since Roman times.

The site was, ironically, next to Lincolnshire's first holiday resort, a place called Freiston Shore, which two centuries ago boasted a fine sandy beach where horse-racing took place and tourists arrived en masse to bathe and drink the seawater for medicinal purposes. However, the rapid silting of The Wash had seen the golden sands gradually turn to salt marsh, leaving the resort with its two big hotels half a mile from the sea. Skegness with its splendid beaches and Great Northern Railway line opened in 1873 boomed in its place.

Freiston eventually received a railway, but it was not linked to the national network. It was a 2ft gauge tramway system was introduced solely to aid the boys build the dykes and turn the marshes into farmland.

Lengths of portable track were laid in place along the sea wall construction sites, and the young offenders pushed the tipper wagons along the railway by hand.

The Borstal railway system fanned out over the reclaimed fens, with a 'main line' running for three miles from North Sea Camp, so named because it started out as exactly that, a tented camp site, to Freiston Shore. Branches turned off at various points to reclamation sites along the way.

The rolling stock mainly comprised hand-operated tipper wagons, while some chassis had been modified to carry winches and water pumps.

The Borstal boys never had the luxury of a steam engine, but eventually the railway brought in four

One of the prison railway's level crossings at Freiston Shore.

Britain's only prison railway was in effect a giant train set, with portable lengths of track laid as required for salt marsh reclamation.

The coast at Freiston Shore today. The 21st century policy is one of 'managed retreat', allowing the sea to take back reclaimed land, and sea defences to build up naturally through the development of salt marsh to take the power out of the incoming tide – effectively unravelling the work of the Borstal boys.

Lister four-wheeled petrol-engined locomotives, a move greatly welcomed by the inmates.

A few hundred yards from Freiston Shore stood the 'dining room', a Nissen-type hut where locomotives and stock were stored, and prisoners working on the reclamation schemes were served hot meals at lunchtime. Until 1970, an insulated container with the cooked lunch for those out on the marsh was transported by flat wagon pushed by two boys.

The railway remained in use until the seventies. In later times, a reconditioned 1953 Priestman Wolf Mark IIIB dragline was used to haul large amounts of mud from the coastline, and there reached the point where the authorities saw no point in reclaiming further mudflats, as greater expansion of the sea defences eastwards might not stand storm surges.

At first the fleet of five locomotives, which by then had been converted from petrol to diesel operation, was placed into store and the temporary track piled high next to the old sea wall at Freiston Shore. One of the locomotives, Lister No 33651 of 1949, and three wagons were taken for preservation at HM Prison College at Newbold Revel near Rugby, where they were placed on open display.

Far left: 'Mallard' of the marshes! One of the prison line's Lister petrol locomotives as delivered.

Left: For some years, HM Prison North Sea Camp displayed one of its railway's locomotives and a rake of tipper wagons at its main entrance.

The young offenders institution became an adult prison, HMP North Sea Camp, in 1988.

Two governors looked at the railway, firstly in the eighties and then in 2002, and drew up schemes to rebuild it, possibly to carry visitors on special open days.

The latter scheme came to grief when the second of the governors parted company with the prison service and the authorities decided to rid themselves of the railway once and for all, selling it off at auction in March 2005. In a final twist to the story, a railway enthusiast who had been hired to help with the planned revival was himself jailed for six months that year for helping a prisoner escape.

Some of the wagons had not moved for so long that they had tree trunks growing through them, while one locomotive had a bird's nest in the engine compartment.

Various enthusiast groups, including the Cleethorpes Coast Light Railway, bought items at bargain prices, and around £17,000 was raised.

It is said that the Tory Peer and novelist Geoffrey Archer was not a railway enthusiast, for otherwise he would have been in his element when he received a four-year stint for perjury, and served part of his sentence at the jail. Instead, while out on a day's work placement in 2002, he attended a private social function in Lincoln, again hitting the tabloid headlines for doing so.

Young offenders 'playing trains' on the shore of The Wash. Would any of them want to see a bucket and spade again, let along steal one?

CHAPTER TWENTY ONE

NO DOUBLE DECKERS – WE'RE BRITISH!

BRITAIN INVENTED THE self-propelled railway locomotive, but has not always been first to adopt major innovations which followed in its wake.

As we saw with the Snowdon Mountain Railway, what is commonplace on the Continent and round the globe is unique in Britain.

The same holds true for double deck trains, a concept widely embraced elsewhere but all but passed over in the UK.

Double deck buses and street trams were a natural progression from the horse bus of the 19th century, and it was logical that the principle could be adapted to railway networks in order to double capacity without adding extra coaches to trains.

A basic double deck carriage type was used on the Bombay, Baroda & Central India Railway in 1862, and two years later, similar vehicles appeared on the Lahore to Amritsar section of the Punjab & Delhi Railway.

A far more sophisticated double deck car was introduced on Copenhagen suburban lines in 1877, and on the Prussian Light Railway from Offenburg to Frankfurt (Main) in 1880.

Bulleid 4DD unit No 4002 heads a commuter service at London Bridge in August 1964.

Around the same time, Berlin workmen were carried in double deck carriages between Grunewald and Westend. The Western Railway of France used them on local services in Paris from 1879, also to avoid having to lengthen platforms.

In North America, the Baltimore & Ohio Railroad pioneered their use. The general pattern around the world was that double deck coaches became more popular as cities expanded from the 1880s onwards, and space for building new lines or extending stations was at a premium.

Britain waited until after World War Two before dabbling with double deckers.

It was the Southern Railway's great Chief Mechanical Engineer, Oliver Bulleid, best known for his streamlined Merchant Navy, Battle of Britain and West Country Pacifics, who designed what was to be the country's only double deck, or 'bilevel', passenger trains.

Overcrowding on rush-hour services from Charing Cross had become infamous and intolerable, and the 5.45pm to Bexleyheath was described as the 'Sardine Special'.

The problem became so bad that even the Government took notice. After it was raised in the House of Commons in 1948, the Parliamentary Secretary to the Minister of Transport said that the solution appeared to be double deck trains, and revealed that the Southern Region was on the case.

Bulleid designed two prototype four-coach double deck third rail pick-up electric multiple unit sets for the Dartford commuter route. They were built at Lancing and Eastleigh works. Unlike Europe and North America, the far more restrictive British loading gauge does not allow for normal double-deck cars with two fully separated decks.

The coaches had alternating high and low level compartments mounted on a standard 62ft

Above left: One of the double deckers built for commuter service in Copenhagen between 1877 and 1901, the last of which was withdrawn in 1936.

Above right: Polish State Railways 2-6-2 No 0149-59 heads from Crodzisk to Wolsztyn with a local stopping train comprising double decker coaches in February 2002. Steam has been retained on this route for use by the Wolsztyn Experience British-led initiative, which keeps heritage traction alive by selling driver courses to foreigners.

Dutch bilevel train at station Amsterdam Bijlmer Arena. The double decker concept all but escaped Britain.

underframe: in bus technology terms, they were not classic double deckers, but more like 'one-and-a-half' deckers.

Each set was made up of two motor coaches and two trailers and contained 22 high and 24 low-level compartments seating 508 persons, with a further 44 tip-up seats, providing a total of 1104 seats when the sets were run as an eight-coach train.

The two sets, Nos 4001-4002, were restricted to the lines between Charing Cross, Cannon Street and Gravesend Central, because of the restrictive British loading gauge, which was especially tight on the former South Eastern & Chatham Railway network.

The first of the sets, designated 4DD (four car double deckers) was officially launched on 1 November 1949 and entered public service the next day. British Railways wisely decided to see how the prototypes performed before committing to a production run.

They were not deemed a success, and in December, 1950, the Southern Region said no more would be built. Passengers complained that they had less room and less comfortable seats, and the ventilation was inadequate.

While more people could travel on double deckers, it was found that because there was just one door to 22 seats, instead of one door to ten or 12 seats as on other suburban stock, boarding and alighting of passengers was desperate during the rush hour. Passengers had to enter via the lower compartment, from which a short stairway led to the upper compartment.

So the Southern Region chose to take the concept no further, and instead looked towards ten-coach trains, with longer platforms – just what Bulleid's designed team had aimed to avoid.

Needing a major overhaul, the sets were withdrawn on 1 October 1971. Enthusiast Esmond Lewis-Evans bought motor coaches Nos 13003 and 13004 from set No 4902 and trailer No 13503 and moved them to his South Eastern Steam Centre, based in the former steam shed at Ashford, Kent. There, without a 750V power supply being available, No 13003 was hauled, bizarrely, by French express Nord compound 4-6-0 No 230D.11 6.

The steam centre closed following a rent dispute with British Rail in 1976, and following legal action, British Rail sold what was left on the site in 1984 to be scrapped, and sadly, No 13503 was cut up.

The motor coaches, however, survived and eventually were reunited at the Northampton Ironstone Railway's Hunsbury Hill base on the outskirts of the town where they are now stored. Sadly neglected by much of the railway restoration movement, their restoration is very much a long-term aim, but as a unique niche in British railway history they are of immense importance and deserve to be saved. In an ideal world, they should be looked after as part of Britain's National Collection.

The idea of double deck trains in Britain did not disappear with the 4DDs. In the early seventies, a proposal for double deck commuter EMUs using single-axle bogies was made, but came to nothing. Around 2005, the Labour Government promised to again look into double deck stock as a way of boosting capacity on commuter routes, while conceding that this time round, the loading gauge would have to be increased.

While walk-through double deck stock, taking advantage of much larger loading gauges, can be found in Europe, Asia, Australia and North America, from branch line sets to SNCF's TCV Duplexes, the only currently suitable British line for such stock is High Speed 1, aka the Channel Tunnel Rail Link. At the time of writing, no proposals have been made for running a double deck service over it.

Maybe if Brunel's broad gauge had been adopted…

Will it ever run again? One of the two surviving 4DD vehicles at Northampton.

CHAPTER TWENTY TWO
FENLAND HARVEST TIME

Steam tram Swift *all set to haul a passenger train around the North Ings Farm Museum circular line.*

The official reopening train on the Lincolnshire Coast Light Railway on 3 May 2009 comprised Major, *a World War Two army surplus Motor Rail Simplex locomotive, which was bought unused by the line in 1960 and given a plywood body built to provide a cab, and restored coach No 22 from Derbyshire's long-defunct Ashover Light Railway, which had previously served as a sports pavilion.*

DURING THE FIRST weekend of September 2010, one of Britain's lesser-known heritage railways celebrated its half centenary. It was in 1958 that a group of enthusiasts made history by starting work on Britain's first full-size railway to be built by volunteer enthusiasts, and on a greenfield site too, as opposed to reviving a closed line.

Not only that, but the Lincolnshire Coast Light Railway offered 'real' public transport as opposed to a living museum for sightseers. Running for a mile at Humberston, near Cleethorpes, and opening on 27 August 1960, it ferried holidaymakers between the Humberston Fitties holiday park and a bus terminus at a time when most people still went to the seaside by train.

The little railway ceased to run at Humberston in the eighties, but after lying dormant for many years, has been moved 25 miles down the coast to a new home a the Skegness Water Leisure Park at Walls Lane, Ingoldmells, where it partially circuits Skegness Aerodrome.

However, its real historical importance lies in the stock it inherited from one of the county's main private railways, and as such offers a window onto some of the most unusual railways ever built in Britain.

Going back again to Richard Trevithick, one of the key points about his invention of the steam locomotive is why he turned from road to rail: the roads of the day were so bad that they struggled to support horses and carts, let alone one of his heavy engines.

The same principal held true in the Lincolnshire fens of the 20th century. The Fenlands are a wholly manmade landscape reclaimed from marshes and the sea, often over many centuries, and long before the Borstal boys set up North Sea Camp!

Once dried out, the peat cracked and shrank, lowering the land below sea level again.

The purpose of reclamation is to create new land for agriculture, and while new roads and farms appeared, in winter or after periods of heavy rain, the peat became soaked and the land reverted to a soggy mass. Both horses and early motor transport faced severe limitations at times like these, and whether a Fenland farm trackway was usable or not could make the vital difference as to whether a crop reached its market.

The Fens are particularly suited to growing potatoes, and as the British railway network expanded, the region became criss-crossed with a web of standard gauge lines, all of which could take the crop to a nationwide market. The problem was – how do you take the crop to the station goods yard from muddy fields?

Taking a leaf from Trevithick, the simple answer was to build a railway of your own.

Early in the 20th century, potato farmer George Caudwell of St Lambert's Hall, Weston near Spalding, laid his own 2ft gauge railway to resounding success.

Such lines became a regular feature of the trenches on the Western Front in World War One. Lightweight petrol-engined locomotives running on temporary tracks were developed not only to keep sparks from steam engines away from ammunition, but to avoid clouds of smoke letting the Hun know exactly where you were.

The end of the conflict released huge quantities of army surplus equipment on to the market: redundant army lorries were used by small entrepreneurs to set up haulage businesses, while the military railway stock was bought up for private use, much of it going to Fenland farmers who laid their own lines across their land in whatever way they chose, without the need for an enabling Act of Parliament as was the case with the 'big' railways.

They served everything from potato fields to pigsties, orchards to greenhouses.

At least 34 of these agricultural railways, with around 110 route miles, were operating in Lincolnshire by the late twenties. Many used only horse traction, while some took the basic military petrol tractors and built crude wooden cabs over them to protect the driver from the merciless wind and rain of the open flatlands.

The biggest system of all was the Nocton Estate Light Railway, its 1ft 11½in gauge system extending to more than 30 miles. Having built an earlier light railway on land at Deeping St Nicholas near Market Deeping in the south of the county, a locality which had many farm railways, W. Dennis & Sons began laying a similar line around the village of Nocton in the

Bill Woolhouse, who founded the original Lincolnshire Coast Light Railway at Humberston, with Paul one of the preserved Simplex locomotives which hauled potato crops over the Nocton Estate Light Railway.

A paraffin-fuelled locomotive, pulling a wagon load of potato sacks on the Dennis Estates system at Deeping St Nicholas, lines up alongside a full-size steam engine at the line transhipment siding.

The only coach that ran on the Nocton Estate Light Railway undergoing a repaint at the Lincolnshire Coast Light Railway's Skegness base

lowlands near Bardney in mid-Lincolnshire. The Nocton Estates Light Railway used several ex-army Simplex locomotives and at one stage owned two steam engines, and was so big that it needed its own team of drivers, guards, tracklayers and railway workshop.

As well as taking potatoes, sugar beet and grain to market, branches of the system served pigsties from which manure was carried to be spread on the fields, and the mill where feed for the cattle and sheep was prepared, and even ran through the middle of tomato greenhouses. It also took coal to the Nocton Pumping Engine which drained the local fen, and supplied water to farms and cottages outside the village which then had no mains supply. It also carried staff such as potato pickers, was used for local Sunday school outings, and in 1927 a van was adapted into a passenger coach for shooting parties.

The railway led to a transhipment siding where produce could be loaded into standard gauge wagons at the main line Nocton & Dunston station.

In 1936 Nocton's main customers, Smith's Potato Crisps, bought the estate along with the railway, which continued to operate for another two decades, alongside lorries. In 1955 it was decided to eliminate transhipment between rail and road wherever possible, so by 1960 much of the railway had closed, although a line served the potato-chitting house until 1969. By then, most of the other Lincolnshire potato railways had long since gone.

In 1958, local enthusiasts obtained redundant stock from the dwindling Nocton line and built a light railway of their own on land leased from Grimsby Rural District Council, and added to the collection over the years. By 1964 the Lincolnshire Coast Light Railway was carrying 60,000 passengers a year, and had obtained a steam locomotive, Peckett 0-4-0 saddle tank No 1008 of 1903 *Jurassic*, which had worked at Southam Limeworks in Warwickshire.

Changing holiday patterns and increased car ownership saw patronage fall sharply in the early eighties, and by 1985 the line could not afford to renew its lease and amongst other difficulties closed...but did not die.

The reborn Lincolnshire Coast Light Railway has won a Heritage Railway Association award for its reopening and conservation of potato railway stock. However, there is still one farm railway running in Lincolnshire, albeit one that was built in 1971, after the others had long since vanished from the face of the county.

The owner of North Ings Farm at Dorrington, north of Sleaford, installed a short 2ft gauge line to serve the chicken sheds, handling feed, eggs and waste. After the poultry side of the business closed a decade later, the railway was still used around the farm, and slowly but surely evolved into a local museum operation, six industrial diesels and a freelance vertical-boilered steam tram engine named *Swift* supplementing the original locomotive and wagons, with the track being extended to form a train-set-style circuit a third of a mile long.

The North Ings Farm Museum is open on the first Sunday of the month during the

Loading potatoes from the three-quarter-mile light railway at J.T. White's farm in Horsepit Lane, Pinchbeck, near Spalding, on to a solid-tyred Thorneycroft lorry in the 1920s. Near right is foreman Bill Hayes, near left is Jack Robinson, while Bill Adcock is on the lorry. This potato railway carried produce to the now-closed Boston-Spalding main line.

The beautifully-restored interior of a World War One ambulance wagon which ran on the Nocton Estates Light Railway, re-equipped with stretchers, and now preserved inside the Lincolnshire Coast Light Railway's stock shed at Skegness.

The Lincolnshire Coast Light Railway's substantial new engine and carriage shed at Skegness Water Leisure Park contains many items of potato railway rolling stock.

summer. Elsewhere, at Vine House Farm, Deeping St Nicholas, now a market-leading producer of wild bird food, has a loading dock from its pre-World War Two 2ft 2in gauge two-mile-long system preserved, along with two of the four flat wagons, while some of the rails can be seen in use to support the roof of a barn.

For those who wish to know more about this fascinating though largely forgotten area of British railway history, Stewart E. Squires' book *The Lincolnshire Potato Railways* published by Oakwood Press is the best place to start.

CHAPTER TWENTY THREE
A BIZARRE RAILWAYS 'THEME PARK'

Lydd station, closed to passengers since the sixties, is still intact, but the now freight-only line that runs through it is not part of the Southern electrified network and has to rely on diesel haulage for nuclear flask trains from Dungeness.

LAND'S END, THE westernmost point of the English mainland, has long been a massive tourist magnet, yet nobody ever built a railway to take passengers there. Similarly, if you want to travel by train to John O'Groats, you have to take the road transport from the nearest railhead, Thurso or Wick, and the most north-easterly point of Scotland, Duncansby Head, is still a mile to go. As for getting to the north-western extremity of the British Isles, Cape Wrath, don't even think about it.

Yet the southern-eastern extremity of Britain is very different indeed, for despite it being a barely-populated desert of marsh and shingle, it has attracted railways like no other place in Britain. Public transport, industrial concerns, military railways, experimental track…many of the people in Dungeness even live in railway carriages.

While Crewe, Swindon, Derby, Darlington and Eastleigh proudly claim to be railway towns because of their historical locomotive works, tiny Dungeness has also entered this very

Pacific No 6 Samson *slows as it approaches the bungalow town of Dungeness, its final destination. The place has a Wild West feel with wooden houses and lines of telegraph poles and you could imagine tumbleweed blowing through the uncultivated shingle gardens.*

elite group – but very much through the back door, and then by sticking a hand up through the cat flap to open the lock.

Yet why would anyone want to build any railway serving this barren and seemingly inhospitable extremity of south-east England in the first place?

The area was first linked to the 'outside world' by rail on 7 December 1881, when the Lydd Railway Company opened a branch from Appledore on the Ashford-Hastings main line to Lydd to passengers, with freight services running on to Dungeness to the south, a section which opened to passengers in April 1883. There had been talk of building a new cross-Channel port at Dungeness – old Norse for 'headland' – but nothing materialised.

The Dungeness branch had its sparse single-platform terminus at the foot of the old lighthouse. Its single weatherboarded building incorporating a ticket office, waiting room, ladies room and toilets. There was a run-around loop for the engine and two sidings, the Admiralty Siding serving a naval signal station and a private siding accessing ballast pits.

The branch was operated by the South Eastern Railway from 16 February 1882, and was extended with a branch that turned north, almost back on itself, from Dungeness to New Romney, and which opened on 19 June 1884. The Lydd Railway Company became part of the South Eastern in January 1895.

Dungeness is a place built on shingle. Indeed, it is one of the biggest expanses of shingle in the world, and its rich flora and fauna, with more than 600 different types of plant and many rare insects, have seen it declared a Site of Special Scientific Interest.

Ancient and modern: Dungeness fisherman's railway, with the giant nuclear power station to the left on the horizon.

Pacific No 2 Northern Chief *waits at Dungeness station, with the new lighthouse in the background.*

The vast expanses of what to many would be wastelands were seen as wonderful by the British army, who decided this would be the perfect spot for a massive army camp and series of firing ranges where there would be nobody around to get in the way.

The soldiers brought much patronage to the line until the end of World War One, although Romney Marsh is really a place where you need a motor car if you want to get around, and passenger numbers tailed off. A standard gauge line was built from Lydd to the first range in 1883, but was lifted in 1927.

With a 1930s boom in holiday traffic along the coast, and new houses being built, the Southern Railway realigned the New Romney branch with a new junction a mile to the south east with new halts at Lydd-on-Sea and Greatstone-on-Sea, reopening the line on 4 July 1937. Lydd station became Lydd Town and passenger services to the lonely outpost of Dungeness were withdrawn, although the line was retained for freight until 1952.

The line received a boost with the building of Dungeness Nuclear Power Station and its opening in 1965. However, Dr Beeching had named the line in his famous report of 1963.

Goods services to New Romney were withdrawn in 1964 and passenger trains on 6 March

1967. Lydd Town remained open for freight until 1967, the branch as far as Romney Junction survived to carry flasks of nuclear waste from Dungeness B power station, although it has carried occasional troop trains and enthusiast railtours, such as the 'Lydd Ranger' on 13 March 2005. Of Dungeness station, only the foundations remain, although the ridge that carried the trackbed can still be made out.

The line could be revived as part of plans by the London Airport Authority to expand tiny Lydd Airport into an international terminus handling more than two million passengers a year, and already renamed London Ashford Airport.

Returning to the army use of the line, the ranges had their own 2ft gauge system laid, which began with just five miles of track, with 15 miles extant in 1990, but has since been drastically reduced.

In 1888 the camp became the testing ground for an acid-based high explosive, later named Lyddite. The first permanent buildings were erected in 1906.

The purpose of the ranges was testing the effectiveness of artillery and new weapons including tanks, which made their appearance during World War One, and also infantry target shooting practice. A military hospital was also set up there during the war. The Lydd Military Railway not only brought in ammunition and supplies but even horses transported in boxvans.

Almost all of its narrow gauge line was laid during World War One on the shingle beach of Denge Marsh, following the contours of the land to provide up and down gradients.

At first, the system was used for target practice, with wood and canvas silhouettes of men and war machinery hauled by Motor Rail and Lister rail tractors at 25mph. After World War Two, D. Wickham & Co of Ware Hertfordshire, better known for manufacturing railway platelayers' trolleys, supplied several self-propelled target-carrying

Flying Scotsman, which went on to become the world's most famous railway locomotive, stands at King's Cross depot in the mid-twenties.

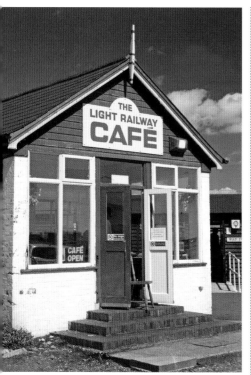

The station café at Dungeness today.

vehicles. So that the soldiers shot the target and not the trolley itself, the engine and axle/chain-drive of each trolley was protected by a heavy armoured steel body.

Once each target vehicle had been prepared and started, the points were set on its intended route and with the brake released, it would set off on its journey minus a driver. At various points it would emerge into the line of vision of soldiers who would fire at it.

A fleet of five Ruston diesel shunters hauled permanent way trains over the system. The tracks south-west of the camp itself were known as Holdstone Run and beyond them to the south as Galloways Run.

Needless to say, the range railways have never been accessible to the public, although examples of stock found their way to Amberley Working Museum in Sussex, the Leighton Buzzard Railway and the Bala Lake Railway.

Not only did the coming of one railway create another and an army camp to boot, but also a 'railway town', for Dungeness today largely comprises homes built from old Victorian wooden-bodied railway carriages, in the shadow of the giant power station.

The Southern Railway owned much land at Dungeness, and once withdrawn from service, the redundant coaches taken there by rail in the 1920s, had the bodies sold off as homes for local fishermen.

More old railway bodies appeared in the fifties as accommodation for the builders of the power station was required: intended as only temporary accommodation, they ended up being permanently inhabited.

Such carriages formed cheap and instant accommodation, especially for do-it-yourself enthusiasts who could make internal and external alterations, boxing in the roofs and then adding chimneys and fireplaces at the rear, followed by lean-to extensions.

Opposite the Britannia pub stands a white bungalow, the shape of the tongue and groove panelling which covers it just about betrays its origins as a railway coach. It was once a royal saloon for no less a figure than Queen Victoria.

Over the decades, the poor man's hovel became the rich man's paradise. Londoners found they could buy the carriage cottages for a snip, and they became trendy weekend retreats, the prices soaring as the years went by. Bought for £10 from the railway, in 2010 some were fetching more than £200,000.

In several cases, top architects and designers stepped in to convert them into stylish and futuristic luxury dwellings, some with the original carriage still inside.

Another example of a short narrow gauge line laid on the shingle at Dungeness was to be found at the Trinity House Experimental Testing Station, set up by the country's lighthouse authority to test different types of fog signal. In 2009, its buildings were also turned into designer homes after being sold off.

Yet all of these railways today pale into obscurity when presented with the locality's most

famous line of all: the 15in gauge Romney, Hythe & Dymchurch Railway was long the world's smallest passenger-carrying line.

It was devised by two men, racing driver, millionaire landowner, former army officer and miniature railway fan Captain Jack Howey and Count Louis Zborowski, a wealthy aristocratic racing driver, who wanted to build a fully-operational main line express railway but in miniature. The locomotives would be scale replicas of main line steam locomotives, and would run on 15in gauge, not 4ft 8½in.

After failing to buy Lakeland's very similar Ravenglass & Eskdale Railway, Zborowski ordered two Pacific locomotives to be designed by the leading model railway engineer of his day, Henry Greenly, and built in Colchester by Davey, Paxman and Co. They were named *Green Goddess*, after the 1921 stage play by William Archer which Howey had enjoyed, and *Northern Chief*.

Zborowski was killed while racing at Monza in the Italian Grand Prix before they could be delivered, leaving Howey with two splendid engines but with nowhere to run them. In a flash of inspiration, Greenly suggested laying a railway along the coast at Romney Marsh.

A double-track line was laid over the eight miles between Hythe and New Romney, the railway's headquarters, and was officially opened on 16 July 1927. It was extended to Dungeness the following year.

It was an instant hit with the public, and trade boomed to the point where soon there were nine miniature versions of main line express Pacific engines hauling trains. It looked like a larger version of a seaside miniature railway, but nonetheless provided, and still does, genuine timetabled public transport.

Above left: *Captain Howey proudly stands at his New Romney station in 1926, with locomotive designer Henry Greenly to the right. Driving* Green Goddess *is none other than Herbert Nigel Gresley, the LNER Chief Mechanical engineer, who later produced world-beating full-size Pacifics like* Flying Scotsman *and* Mallard.

Above right: *However, Sir Nigel Gresley, as he later became, is not believed to have played any part whatsoever in the design of this redundant-looking locomotive on one of the Dungeness fish railways.*

A Lydd Ranges railway target wagon, now in the care of the Leighton Buzzard Railway.

The pre-radar Denge acoustic mirrors still stand, but are no longer rail connected.

The Romney, Hythe & Dymchurch also spawned a branch line, which became all but a railway unto itself. Never carrying public passengers, it was built by the military as part of an early invasion warning device.

The line was built in 1929 at the request of the War Department, curving away inland south of Romney Sands station to serve a secret military installation working on acoustic aircraft detection at Denge. Its terminus was known as War Department Halt.

There a series of huge concrete dishes was constructed, the purpose of which was to concentrate the noise from aircraft approaching from across the Channel. Bizarre as the structure seems today, it really did work to a point – but the project was rendered obsolete by the development of radar.

The War Department had its own petrol-engined locomotive, and ran daily staff trains from Hythe to War Department Halt. Uniquely in the world of 'tourist' railways, the army even produced its own 15in gauge armoured troop train for use on the coastal route during World War Two. Romney, Hythe & Dymchurch locomotive No 5 *Hercules* was fitted with plating and ran with two plated trucks to patrol the line. It was the only miniature armoured train in the world. Bizarre, yes, but certainly effective, serving a part of Britain that was closest to Nazi-occupied Europe..

The railway was also used during the building of PLUTO (Pipe Line Under The Ocean) to provide fuel for the Allied invasion of Normandy in June 1944. After the war, the railway took over the military branch, using it for freight-only services, transporting shingle to Hythe where it was transferred to road transport. This traffic lasted until 1951, and the branch was lifted that winter. The locomotive survived and was rebuilt as the line's PW2 Scooter track maintenance and shunting engine.

There was another and even shorter-lived freight branch of the Romney, Hythe & Dymchurch Railway, laid in 1937 to the east of the main line near Dungeness, running for over a quarter of a mile to the beach, for the purpose of carrying fish. Platform 1 at Hythe was extended to accommodate four-wheel fish wagons, with the catch being taken on by road, but the venture, started after the standard gauge line to Dungeness was axed in 1937, was unsuccessful.

However, its short life led to perhaps the most bizarre of all the many types of railway at Dungeness.

Local fisherfolk not only had the railway concept to thank for their accommodation in the form of the old carriages, but also for their day-to-day income.

Looking at the Romney, Hythe & Dymchurch fish trade branch, they realised that the best way of dragging their catch from their boats on the high shingle ridge overlooking the sea to the coastal road alongside the beach was by rail. Today, you can still see several very much home-made 15in gauge railways, some hundreds of yards long, rusting away, some having

once had the luxury of home-made motive power, embankments, viaducts and bridges to cross dips in the shingle, but most of them fell into disuse by the early 21st century, being replaced by concrete walkways and matting pathways.

The Hythe to New Romney section of the miniature railway reopened to the public in 1946, while Romney to Dungeness section followed a year later, Laurel and Hardy cutting the ribbon. However, wartime deterioration led to the New Romney to Dungeness section being permanently reduced to single line only,

The Romney, Hythe & Dymchurch Railway is licensed by the Post Office for rail postal services, and is allowed to issue its own postage stamps. A four-wheel secure postage wagon was built, and several first-day covers have been issued. The railway operates a parcels service, whereby parcels can be ferried from one station to another.

Dungeness station is rare in having a balloon-like loop so that incoming trains can go out again without the locomotive having to be turned or run backwards.

The station and its restaurant stand in the shadow of Dungeness Old Lighthouse, the fourth on the headland, built in 1901 and replaced in 1961 by its black-and-white striped successor to the east. The 1901 lighthouse is now open as a tourist attraction, and if you climb the 169 steps to the top you can enjoy sweeping panoramas of Romney Marsh as the little train below chugs off into the distance on what seems a thread of cotton, all but lost amidst the great shingle waste that is Dungeness, the world's most unlikely but richly-varied railway village.

End of the line: the freight-only Lydd branch leads to this transhipment siding where diesel-hauled trains collect nuclear flasks from Dungeness B power station.

CHAPTER TWENTY FOUR
COLD WAR CITY

The eastern portal of Box Tunnel in GWR days, with the freight spur leading through a separate tunnel into Tunnel Quarry on the right.

Ruston diesel shunter WD1, built in 1936 and seen underground in 2002, was used for moving heavy ammunition through the subterranean complex.

ONE OF THE GREATEST feats of early railway engineering was undoubtedly the construction of Isambard Kingdom Brunel's Box Tunnel. The great engineer used a team of 1200 navvies to confound his critics yet again and dig through Box Hill, the biggest obstacle that lay between Chippenham and Bath on the route of his Great Western Railway from Paddington to Bristol.

Working around the clock from September 1836, 247,000 cubic yards of spoil were excavated, and it was estimated that 100 labourers lost their lives in the primitive working conditions. The 9636ft tunnel, then the longest on any railway in Britain, reached the stage where one out of two tracks was ready for use on 30 June 1841, completing the entire route, with trains taking four hours for the whole journey as opposed to days by stagecoach.

On 29 August 1949, the Soviet Union tested its first fission bomb, nicknamed Joe 1 by the USA, which was shocked at how much further ahead the USSR had been in its nuclear weapons research than had previously been thought.

In November 1958, Soviet Premier Nikita Khrushchev delivered a speech in which he demanded that the USA, United Kingdom and France pull their forces out of West Berlin within six months. This demand sparked a three year crisis over the future of the city of Berlin that culminated in 1961 with the building of the Berlin Wall. In October 1962, the world tottered on the brink of nuclear war as the Americans confronted the Soviets in the Cuban missile crisis.

Enter a James bond film script writer. A secret underground city far away from London to house the Government and the Royal Family in the event of a nuclear war had been built, accessed by a secret passageway leading off from a railway tunnel. The city could accommodate thousands of people living, working and spending their recreational time there, for months if not years, safe from the fallout from any nuclear strike. Of course, the rest of the population would be told nothing about its existence.

Add in a touch of the conspiracy theory. For many years an urban myth persisted amongst the enthusiast fraternity that following the end of British Railways steam in 1968, rather than being sent to the scrapyard many locomotives had been buried beneath Salisbury Plain as a 'strategic reserve', to reappear in a time of global crisis when diesel fuel was in short supply,

At the main internal platform, munitions were loaded onto a conveyor belt for distribution within the subterranean ammunition store.

The underground transhipment station in military use, with standard gauge box vans lined up alongside the platform.

or when the detonation of a nuclear bomb had wiped out the electronic circuits needed to make diesel locomotives operate…

So where is the link to Brunel? While boring Box Trunnel, the navies stumbled on rich veins of freestone, highly prized as a very attractive building material. Accordingly, nearby Corsham became a boom town as the stone was mined and quarried, with nearly 1000 people engaged in the industry by late Victorian times, the stone being taken out by the GWR… through a standard gauge freight branch running directly off the main line at the eastern portal of Box Tunnel into the great underground caverns that had been created by the miners.

The mines were exhausted by the 1920s, but with Hitler's rise to power in Germany, in 1936 a new use was found for the Ridge, Tunnel and Eastlays quarries by the War Office, for use as an underground munitions depot. By 1943, Corsham's Central Ammunition Depot, as it became known, was the focal point of 125 acres of subterranean chambers containing 300,000 tons of explosives and munitions, not only at Box Tunnel but in separate underground quarries throughout the Bath region.

The freight spur from the tunnel portal into the the 50-acre Tunnel Quarry was upgraded for military use. Complete with a 750ft underground platform and refuge sidings, it ran for around 2000ft underground. Inside the caverns, it led to a 2ft gauge internal railway system

Ammunition was transported around the complex on these 2ft gauge wagons.

Railway tunnels diverge in the underground complex.

with its own diesel locomotives, turntables, engine houses and workshops serving the gigantic ammunition store, which was divided into 'districts'.

Three Hunslet 0-6-0 diesel shunters, chosen because they would not emit sparks in the ammunition dump, worked the standard gauge line, taking wagons to and from the reception sidings at the GWR's Thingley Junction three miles away.

Daily maintenance of the locomotives was conducted at the underground locomotive shed.

Whitehall spread rumours that the Ministry of Food was building an emergency food dump to cover up the real purpose of the caverns.

At the outbreak of World War Two, many RAF command centres were located underground, No 10 Fighter Command covering the West Country found a ready home in Brown's Quarry, an offshoot of Tunnel Quarry. In 1940, the extensive Spring Quarry, on the other side of Brunel's tunnel from Tunnel Quarry, was converted by the Ministry of Air Production into what was described as "the largest underground factory in the world." There, the Bristol Aircraft Company turned out Centaurus engines while a separate part was occupied by BSA for making gun barrels.

Aircraft company chairman Sir Reginald Verdon Smith commissioned professional artist Olga Lehmann to decorate the Spring Quarry canteen areas with vivid floor-to-ceiling murals. Over 40 of these survive today.

These shadow factories, however, turned out to be a white elephant, for by the time they opened in early 1943, Luftwaffe bombing was a much-diminished threat.

Yet the £20-million spent on adapting the caverns would not be wasted. The network of quarries became a focal point of Cold War planning.

Originally codenamed, SUBTERFUGE, in the early sixties the Corsham caverns, including over 60 miles of internal roads and covering 35 acres 100ft below the town, were converted into an office for Prime Minister Harold Macmillan, the war cabinet and chiefs of staff, and possibly the Royal Family, under the codename BURLINGTON (and finally TURNSTILE). It was said that the Barracks Hill complex as it was known could house up to 4000 central Government staff.

The ammunition depot's underground conveyor belt used to transport munitions from railway lines to the stores.

Artist Olga Lehmann was hired to decorate some of the underground depot's canteen areas with vivid floor-to-ceiling murals.

The New York grid-style city of roads and avenues was fitted out with all the facilities essential for survival, such as underground hospitals, laboratories canteens, kitchens and laundries to storerooms of supplies, accommodation areas, offices and a bar.

An underground lake and treatment plant could provide all the drinking water needed whilst 12 huge tanks could store the fuel required to keep four massive generators in the underground power station, running for three months.

The city also had the second largest telephone exchange in Britain and a BBC studio from which the Prime Minister could address the nation. Many of the civil servants who had secretly been allocated a desk there knew nothing whatsoever about the existence of the city.

The Emergency Government War Headquarters, as it was designated, was last upgraded in the early years of the Thatcher government, when the Soviet Union invaded Afghanistan in yet another east-west micro-conflict by proxy, but glasnost, the fall of the Berlin Wall, the rise of Boris Yeltsin as Russian president, the break-up of the Soviet Union and the demise of communism rendered the city obsolete.

In December 2008, left with just four staff, the site was finally decommissioned. Subsequently, much of the complex has now been mothballed or sold, parts of it being used for commercial storage, although a RAF and military communications base remains. The entrance from Box Tunnel is now bricked up.

Amongst the disused offices and stores are reminders of the Cold War era, such as shelving with signs GAS, BIO and ATOM. A 2ft gauge Hunslet four-wheeled diesel, WD1, which ran on the internal system, is still underground.

There was no hidden reserve of steam locomotives: the ones the conspiracy theorists said had never reached the scrapyards had been cut up after all, and the records of what had happened had been simply incomplete.

That did not stop three men entering Box Tunnel in September 2003 looking for the entrance, and ending up in court after causing six-hour delays to main line services while they were rescued.

English Heritage has photographed much of what remains and is advising on the management of both the surface and underground structures, which are rapidly deteriorating through damp and lack of maintenance, and there is the debate as to whether the complex should be preserved as part of the nation's history, just like a Roman fort or Norman castle.

CHAPTER TWENTY FIVE

THE WIGHT PLACE TO RETIRE

OLD LONDON UNDERGROUND trains don't die. They are simply shipped over to the Isle of Wight for a new life beside the sea.

Secondhand rolling stock forming the mainstay of rail traffic on the island is by no means a post-steam era phenomenon, for it has been happening from Victorian times.

The pre-Grouping Isle of Wight Central Railway purchased redundant A1X 'Terrier' 0-6-0 tank engines from the London Brighton & South Coast Railway, while the Southern Railway despatched London & South Western Railway O2 0-4-4 tank locomotives across The Solent when they were made obsolete by the electrification of London suburban lines. 'Terriers' and O2s became synonymous with the island's rail network both up to the end of steam, and in the heritage era, with the establishment of the Isle of Wight Steam Railway.

At one time, Wight had a labyrinthine network of railway lines to serve it seemed almost every corner, but the mass closures of the sixties swept all that remained away, barring part of one route: the 8½-mile Ryde Pier to Shanklin section of the Ryde Pier-Ventnor line, retained to serve the resorts on the east coast.

British Railways had wanted to close everything apart from the Ryde Pier section, which would take ferry passengers from one end of the pier to the other. Local campaigners forced a compromise with Ryde-Shanklin remaining open. Why the entire line could not have been saved through to Ventnor remains a permanent subject for debate.

No more taking city gents to work, but Vintage Class 483 1938 underground stock tube trains restored to London Transport livery still give excellent services on the Island Line.

Two London Underground 1938 Standard tube stock units adorned in 'dinosaur' livery pass at Sandown station in April 2001.

Island Line Class 483 No 483002 and 483007 in London Underground livery 'on shed' at Ryde Electric Depot.

One of the original Class 485 Wight tube trains in British Rail blue and grey livery at Ryde Esplanade.

In 1955, the British Railways Modernisation Plan demanded that steam would be phased out in favour of diesel and electric traction as quickly as possible. That would include the remaining railway on the island, not only as a point of principle in order to impose the 'one size fits all' policy, but out of physical necessity.

Steam trains were withdrawn from Ryde Pier on 17 September, and the whole line on 31 December 1966, after which the line was closed to allow 750V third-rail electrification to take place. At the same time, it was decided to increase the height of the trackbed in Esplanade Tunnel, to reduce flooding by very high tides and the need to pump out seawater afterwards at great cost.

The diminished clearance would no longer allow trains built to the national loading gauge to run beneath it, so rolling stock built to a lower height was required. The secondhand market yet again provided the answer: use London Underground tube trains rather than the mainland's Southern Region electric multiple units.

While the line was closed, Ryde Pier Head station was rebuilt and Ryde Esplanade station substantially modified. Services resumed on 20 March 1967 with platform heights adjusted to accommodate the tube trains.

The island's 'new' trains were six four-car refurbished EMUS built for the London Electric Railway from 1923-31 as Standard tube stock. Each unit was formed of a driving motor, two intermediate trailers, and a second driving motor.

Showing their age, around the same time, one was sent to the Science Museum.

Initially classified Class 452 and numbered 041-046, the Wight EMUs were later reclassified Class 485 and numbered 485041-046.

At the outset, they wore all-over BR blue livery with the double arrow logo, changing to standard blue/grey livery in the 1970s, and Network SouthEast's blue livery with red and white stripes in 1986.

Adhering to the Southern Region's numerical classification for EMU types, the four-car sets became 4VEC, and three-car sets 3TIS. When run together as a seven-coach train, they became VECTIS, the Roman name for the island.

The residents welcomed the secondhand trains, as the electrification allowed the line speed to be raised from 40mph to 45mph, providing a more frequent service.

However, taken out of the London Underground tunnels, the units rusted badly in the salty air. From 1989 onwards, they were replaced by 20 Metro-Cammell 1938 tube stock cars, introduced as Class 483 two-car sets but running in formations of up to three pairs. The last 485s were withdrawn from service in 1992 and five vehicles were returned to London Underground for eventual restoration as part of an operational Standard stock museum heritage unit.

Following the privatisation of Britain's railways, in 1996 the Ryde-Shanklin line became the Island Line franchise, won by the Stagecoach Group, with services still branded as Island Line.

No need to duck for this pair of Class 483 tube trains, negotiating the lowered clearance at Ryde Tunnel without a second thought.

A 1938 tube train runs along Ryde Pier.

LSWR 0-4-4T W24 Calbourne ran on the island's lines in the steam age, and completed its latest overhaul in July 2010 ready to re-enter service on the Isle of Wight Steam Railway.

Here comes the ultimate irony, From 2000 onwards, the remaining five 483 units were overhauled, and several of them were repainted into a new livery of blue and yellow…with pictures of dinosaurs on the sides. Intended to represent the internationally-famous fossil riches of the island and its geology, it also highlighted the trains' true place in transport history.

The vehicles were later repainted into the original London Transport red livery, with the additional of yellow warning panels on the cab.

The unusual sight of secondhand London Underground trains running public services on an island is not unique to Wight. In the Channel Islands, the two-mile Alderney Railway has two examples of 1956 tube stock hauled by diesel shunters as passenger trains.

At the Island Line's midway station of Smallbrook Junction, passengers can change trains for the Isle of Wight Steam Railway, which runs on five miles of the old Ryde-Newport line from there as far as Wootton. Its flagship locomotive, 1891-built O2 W24 *Calbourne*, returned to steam in July 2010 after a major overhaul.

'Heritage' does not automatically equate with steam, even though the word automatically suggests it in a railway context. The term could equally as well be applied to the sole remaining part of the national network south of The Solent.

The difference gets all the more confusing if you look at the Lymington branch, which serves ferries bound for the Isle of Wight.

One of the last two Southern Region slam-door units to run in timetabled main line service in Britain, No 1497 crosses heathland en route from Brockenhurst to Lymington in 2007.

Ageing passenger stock not only runs on the Isle of Wight but until 2010, also ran to it. South West Trains' 3-CIG unit No 1497 heads towards Lymington Pier station.

This 5½-mile line from Brockenhurst Junction opened in 1858 and eventually became part of the Southern third-rail system. In the early 21st century, it was decreed that all traditional slam-door stock on the old Southern Region was to be phased out by November 2005 in favour of modern EMUs.

However, South West Trains obtained special dispensation to continue using slam-door stock on the branch on the grounds that it was too short to justify investment in replacement new Class 450 Desiro EMUs, trains ran only at low speeds and central door locking and other safety features could be fitted.

Two Class 421 4-CIG units were bought and refurbished, exclusively to operate services on the line. They were numbered 1497 and 1498, one repainted into Southern Region green and the other into British Rail blue and grey, and officially named *Freshwater* and *Farringford* respectively at a ceremony at Brockenhurst on 12 May 2005. Cut down to three-car units, they were reclassified as 3-CIG, and permission to use them until they were considered life expired in 2013 was granted. The branch was also rebranded as the 'Heritage Line' but there was not a volunteer, a standard feature of such operations, in sight!

In 2009, South West Trains announced plans to replace the pair with Class 158 Sprinters on weekdays and Class 450s. The final 3Cig service left from Lymington Pier at 22.14 on 22 May 2010 and arrived at Brockenhurst at 22.24.

One of the units, No. 1498, now has a new home on the Epping Ongar Railway, London's closest standard gauge operational heritage railway, which in summer 2012 launched a new public steam service. While there are no longer electric rails on the former London Underground branch, and it has to be used only as locomotive-hauled stock, its electric apparatus has been retained intact in the event it might be recertified for main line use for special occasions in the future.

CHAPTER TWENTY SIX
FLOATING ON AIR

AS THE YEARS OF post-war austerity came to an end, many saw technology as the path to the long promised brave new world. The space race was grabbing the imagination, with rockets pointing the way to the moon and maybe beyond, and it seemed that sooner rather than later, everyone would benefit from new futuristic forms of transport. Like the hovercraft, for instance. Like Trevithick's steam locomotive, a thoroughly British invention.

Aero and marine engineering company and flying boat builder Saunders-Roe Limited, based at Columbine Works in East Cowes on the Isle of Wight, demonstrated the Saunders-Roe Nautical 1 (SR-N1), the first hovercraft built to inventor Christopher Cockerell's design, on 11 June 1959. Two weeks later, it crossed the English Channel from Calais to Dover, paving the way for a series of similar air-cushioned sea craft to be built.

It was inevitable that the question would be asked – if it works on sea, why not on land? And could it be adapted to create a new form of railway?

Britain's only hovertrain, RTV31, is preserved at Railworld.

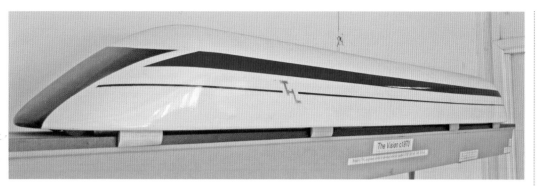

Above left: *The shape of things not to come: a scale model of the proposed British hovertrain.*

Above right: *Members of Hovercraft Development Ltd & Hovercar at Hythe, Hampshire, in 1966. They are, left to right, Ernie Needham, Alan Bing, Mike Charity, Dennis Bliss, Mike Stockford, Geoff Easton, Dave Hammet and Barry Hart. The model, demonstrated at Hovershow '66, is now in the Railworld Museum.*

Several attempts were made to adopt air cushion technology for use in fixed track systems, taking advantage of lower frictional forces to produce high speeds. In France Aérotrain, an experimental high speed hovertrain, was operated between 1965 and 1977 when it was scrapped due to lack of funding and the adoption of the alternative TGV by the French government as its high-speed rail solution.

In England, a short test track was built by Tracked Hovercraft Ltd at Earith, between the Old Bedford River and the smaller Counter Drain in the Cambridgeshire fens.

The hovertrain concept had originated with English engineer Professor Eric Laithwaite (14 June 1921–27 November 1997) of Imperial College, London, who developed an interest in linear induction motors. In the late forties, he demonstrated the first full-size working model of such a motor.

His ideas were finally put into practice with RTV31, the prototype for a tracked hovercraft rail system at Earith. The vehicle used linear magnetic motors for forward motion, and a cushion of air powered from giant fans to lift itself off the track, was built for the tests.

From a standing start it reached 104mph over a mile on 7 February 1973. Yet funding for the project was cancelled a week later by the Heath Government's Aerospace Minister Michael Heseltine. The system was considered to be too expensive for commercial use.

MP Airey Neave and others accused Heseltine of misleading the House of Commons by stating that the Government was still considering backing for the hovertrain project, despite the fact that the Cabinet had already decided otherwise.

The engineering firm Alfred McAlpine took over parts of the project, but despite its efforts, it was finally abandoned in the mid 1980s.

In parallel with his tracked hovercraft rail system, Laithwaite was developing another form of hovertrain, based around magnetic levitation. It became known as Maglev.

Another form of wheel-less train, Maglev trains use powerful electro-magnets to lift itself off its track, whereas RTV31 used a cushion of air.

The Maglev system in operation at Birmingham International Airport.

One of the two British Maglev cars is now the centrepiece of a flowerbed at Peterborough's Railworld Museum. All that now hovers are the bumble bees around it.

JR-Maglev is a magnetic levitation train system developed by the Central Japan Railway Company and Railway Technical Research Institute. The JR-Maglev train comprises a maximum five cars to run on the Yamanashi Maglev Test Line. On 2 December 2003, a three-car train reached 361mph, a world speed record for railed vehicles, in a manned run.

A pair of Maglev vehicles entered commercial service in Britain in 1984, on a 1969ft elevated line linking the then-new Birmingham International Airport terminal to Birmingham International railway station. The driverless cars 'flew' at a height of 15mm and each carried up to 40 passengers with their luggage.

The system was developed as a result of experimental work at the British Rail Research Division laboratory in Derby, and had been commissioned by the Government.

It was eventually taken out of service not because there was anything wrong with the system, but because it proved difficult to get spare parts, and there were numerous breakdowns leaving passengers stranded mid-line.

Maglev was replaced in 2003 by the AirRail Link people mover cable-hauled system using the same guideway.

Eventually, RTV31 and Maglev would come together. At Railworld, the railway museum next to the Nene Valley Railway in Peterborough, RTV31 takes pride of place astride a saved section of the concrete test track at the entrance. Inside, placed firmly in a flower bed with no chance of levitation, sits a Maglev car. Its sister vehicle is inside the Great Hall of the National Railway Museum at York.

While, like Bulleid's double deckers, Maglev failed to take off in the UK long term, the concept has been warmly embraced by other countries.

In Japan, the development of the JR-Maglev by Japan Railways Group began in 1969 and in 2003 it reached a speed of 361mph in tests. The Central Japan Railway Company intends to start a commercial Maglev service between Tokyo and Nagoya in 2025.

The world's first commercial automated urban Maglev system, a 5½-mile line between Tobu and Kyuryo in Aichi opened in March 2005 and has a top speed of 62 mph.

German firm Transrapid built the world's first operational high-speed conventional Maglev railway, the 18¾-mile Shanghai Maglev Train from downtown Shanghai to Pudong International Airport, the first services running in 2002 and a speed of 311mph having been obtained.

The development of the original Maglev design is still continuing in earnest in the USA, Germany and the Far East, with prototype systems being produced. Yet although it was widely mooted for a new trunk high-speed railway linking London to Scotland, in 2010 the Labour Government announced that traditional rail technology would be used instead. So another British invention benefits everyone else.

CHAPTER TWENTY SEVEN
AN AXE BEYOND BEECHING

IF YOU LOOK AT the list of preserved railways in Britain today, there are several modern-day narrow gauge lines which have been laid on old standard gauge trackbeds.

Some lines might not have paid their way under British Railways, but some were so scenic that they were too good to close. One example is the Bala Lake Railway, a 2ft gauge line running alongside the southern shore of Llyn Tegid, one of the most beautiful inland stretches of water in Britain. It occupies the trackbed of the Great Western Railway's route from Ruabon to Dolgellau which closed in the sixties.

Other narrow gauge lines laid on standard gauge trackbeds to form tourist attractions include the Bure Valley, Launceston Steam, Brecon Mountain, Lappa Valley and Kirklees Light railways, so that in itself is nothing unusual.

One line, however, is truly different from the rest – East Devon's Seaton Tramway.

Occupying much of the trackbed of the former Seaton branch, it not only provides public transport but has kept open the rail route along the beautiful estuary of the River Axe as a tourist attraction.

Car 11 runs along the Seaton Tramway which offers spectacular views of the Axe estuary and its birdlife.

Passengers boarding at Colyton.

Cars 2 and 8 alongside each other at Colyton.

Street trams through the countryside rather than an urban area? That may sound bizarre to many people, but it gets better. The trams have been reduced in size by careful rebuilding so that they are only about two thirds the size of the originals. The Seaton Tramway is truly different from the rest!

It was the arrival of the Seaton & Beer Railway in 1868 which turned Seaton into a busy holiday resort, and it was the post-Beeching closure of the branch line later operated by the London & South Western and Southern railways, on 7 March 1966, which dealt a blow to town's seasonal trade. While around 1200 passengers rode on the line on summer Saturdays, a healthy figure in itself, less than a dozen made the final trip, highlighting the fact that winter services were unsustainable.

This unique attraction originated with a manufacturer of milk floats and other battery-electric vehicles. Claude Lane, owner of the Lancaster Electrical Company in Barnet, North London, was a tram enthusiast and in 1949 he built a 15in gauge tram based on former Darwen Tramway Car 23, then running on the Llandudno & Colwyn Bay system. Claude was surprised at how popular his miniature tram became when he ran it at fêtes and other special events. He operated it for a summer season at St Leonards in Sussex, in 1951 and for five seasons at Rhyl from 1952.

In 1953, Claude leased a permanent site at Eastbourne in 1953, and set up a new company, Modern Electric Tramways Ltd, to operate it.

His 2ft gauge Eastbourne Electric Tramway ran for two-thirds of a mile between Princes Park and the Crumbles and his factory manufactured a larger open-top tram, Car 6, also based on the open-top design of Llandudno & Colwyn Bay vehicles, to run on it. It was followed in 1958 by the similar Car 8, in 1961 by Car 4, which was based on a Blackpool Tramways 'open boat' design, and in 1964 by Car 2, based on based on a London Metropolitan Tramways design.

When Eastbourne's road system expanded and left little room for his tramway, Claude began looking for a site of his own.

He heard that the Seaton branch was earmarked for closure and after lengthy negotiations, British Railways agreed to sell him the trackbed, on condition he received a Transfer Order and a Light Railway Order.

Several local residents opposed his plan, claiming at a public inquiry that his trams would

Car 9 passing the Riverside Depot.

Below left: *Car 6 at the Seaton terminus.*

Below right: *Car 14 inside the depot.*

Above left: *The restored but reduced Exeter Tramways Car 19 in Riverside Depot.*

Above right: *Pointwork at Riverside Depot, set into brick paving street-tram style.*

create unacceptable noise and harm the natural beauty of the Axe valley. Seaton Town Council argued that the tramway would become a major asset to the local economy, and Claude won the day.

From September 1969, the complete Eastbourne system had to be dismantled, transported 100 miles westwards and reassembled before the 1970 holiday season ended. Claude and his assistant Allan Gardner made 36 return lorry journeys between Eastbourne and Seaton. The new line was built to a gauge of 2ft 9ins. Already in 1969, Claude had built Car 8 to larger proportions than its predecessors in readiness for the wider track.

On 28 August 1970, Car 8 became the first tram to run in passenger service on the line, taking power from a battery car as overhead wires had yet to be installed. A depot at Riverside just north of the original Seaton branch station, which was demolished following closure, was installed so that during the following winter, the existing trams could be regauged.

At the same time the line was laid as far as Colyford, the midway point, but before the first full season could start, Claude died from a heart attack on 2 April 1971.

Allan Gardner took over as managing director to complete the project with the aid of volunteers. A railway locomotive as opposed to a tram returned to the Seaton branch in the shape of a diesel shunter bought to assist works Car 02 in hauling equipment.

Passing loops were installed at Axmouth and Swan's Nest, allowing trams to operate simultaneously. During 1973 overhead wire and fittings were installed, and the first tram powered from the overhead lines ran that September.

With Seaton's railway station demolished and the site no longer available, land was bought to lay a new trackbed to a fresh terminus site next to Harbour Road car park, and was ready in May 1975. However, flood damage in 1978 delayed the final extension to Colyton until 1980.

Attention afterwards switched to expanding the fleet. Firstly, Metropolitan Tramways Car

94, obtained by Claude in 1962, was reduced in size by cutting the body lengthways in half and narrowing it by 2ft. It entered service in 1984 as enclosed single deck saloon Car 14, and was launched into traffic by the late comedian Larry Grayson. Original Bournemouth Tramways Car 106 was similarly reduced and appeared in 1992 as Car 16.

In 1998, Exeter Tramways Car 19, which ran in the nearby city from 1906 until the system closed in 1931, was cut down in size restored from derelict. More new trams followed in the 21st century in the form of Cars 9, 10 and 11, all of a hybrid design based on Plymouth and Blackburn prototypes.

There are now sufficient trams in all shapes and sizes, from open double-deckers with basic wooden seats to luxuriously-upholstered wood-panelled cars to run a service every few minutes in the high season. More than 100,000 visitors a year nowadays ride along the Axe Valley route, a line that re-emerged phoenix-like from the Beeching Axe but in a somewhat different form.

Part of the appeal is the rich variety of bird life along the estuary, and special services are often run to view it. The original station building at Colyton survives, and has been tastefully adapted into a continental-style terminus complete with a souvenir shop and restaurant facilities.

A scheme to extend the tramway further towards the town centre has been mooted. However, no attempt has been made to extend the line further north along the rest of the old branch to Seaton Junction on the Waterloo-Exeter main line, a question frequently raised by visitors.

The Seaton Tramway did have one locomotive. This four-wheeled Ruston Hornsby diesel shunter was built in 1959 for North Devon Clay ay Torrington, and in 1972 was acquired by the tramway for tracklaying purposes. It has not run since 1981, and has since been donated to the Devon Railway Centre at Cadeleigh station near Tiverton. There it remains on static display pending restoration, and has been named Claude *after the founder of the tramway.*

CHAPTER TWENTY EIGHT
WHERE NO MAN HAS GONE BEFORE

The Americans reached the moon – but British Rail's patented space vehicle aimed to take us to the stars.

ON 19 JUNE 1965, eye-witness reports from Weston-super-Mare and Bristol of a 'flying train' in the sky received much local press coverage. A British Rail spokesman denied that any of its trains were flying that day.

The Bristol Channel is not that far from the military town of Warminster, which became internationally famous in the early to mid-sixties for its UFO sightings. Indeed, only 16 days earlier, after a month in which other local sightings were reported, a glowing cigar-shaped object was seen hovering over Warminster.

When the journalist writing up the story about the 'flying train' sighting rang British Rail for a comment, I remain sceptical as to whether the press officer who answered really bothered to check with his superiors as to whether there was any logical explanation connected with the railway. I certainly would not have done so.

However, just over five years later, asking such a question of British Rail might not have been that wide of the mark…

The sixties had very much been pre-occupied by the Race to the Moon, won by the US with the Apollo 11 landing on 20 July 1969. While the Americans and Russians had been competing to develop space technology, much of the rest of the world could only dream about one day exploring beyond our planet. The fifties saw an explosion in the genre of science fiction, with interstellar travel providing much inspiration for an endless series of movies and comics and eventually the small screen. *Dr Who* with its Daleks, which invaded London in flying saucers, was one of the biggest British TV hits of the period, while *Star Trek* debuted in the US in 1966 and in the UK three years later.

After the lunar landings, it seemed to all that the space age had arrived, and the human race really did have access to the final frontier, where no man had gone before. Many thought it would be just a matter of time before the moon was colonised, man landed on Mars, toured the solar system and maybe ventured to the next star. Fact and fiction were merging fast, or so it seemed.

Harsh reality proved to be very different. Moon landings did not become commonplace: the last took place on 7 December 1972. The Apollo programme was cancelled due to government cutbacks and the NASA exploration programme instead concentrated on the

How British Rail might have adapted a classic science fiction movie poster from 1950.

development of the space shuttle and unmanned probes.

However, those who shared the view that the space age was here to stay included some people either in, or connected with, British Rail.

For on 1 December 1970, a patent application for nothing less than a flying saucer was filed by Jensen and Son on behalf of the British Railways Board. Furthermore, it was granted on 21 March 1973, with the number 1310990.

Before I continue, let me reassure you – as far as this document is concerned – this is a true story, not a conspiracy theory or figment of some wild railway enthusiast's imagination. The document was officially lodged at the Patent Office in London, and the paperwork is indeed there to be examined at the European Patents Office.

The craft, known simply as a space vehicle, was designed by inventor Charles Osmond Frederick.

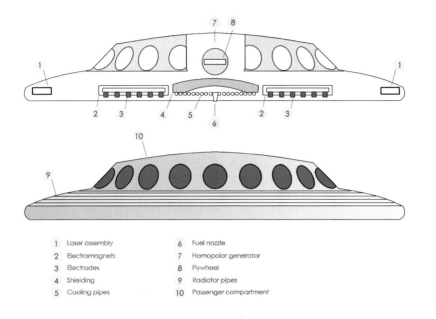

1	Laser assembly	6	Fuel nozzle
2	Electromagnets	7	Homopolar generator
3	Electrodes	8	Flywheel
4	Shielding	9	Radiator pipes
5	Cooling pipes	10	Passenger compartment

The plans for the British Rail patented flying saucer.

It was first conceived as a "raisible platform", intended to compete with services on the East Coast Main Line between London and Edinburgh, at a time when air travel as far as the ordinary family was concerned was still a luxury.

The idea soon evolved into much more, and by the time the patent application had been lodged, it had been transformed into no less than a large passenger vessel for interplanetary travel, powered by "controlled thermonuclear fusion reaction".

Its design was based around the concept of nuclear fusion, using laser beams to produce pulses of nuclear energy in a generator in the centre of the craft.

The pulses of energy would be diverted to a series of radial electrodes running beneath the saucer, turning the energy into electricity which would feed a ring of powerful electromagnets. In turn, these would accelerate subatomic particles emitted by the fusion reaction, providing lift and thrust.

A patent document reads: "The present invention relates to a space vehicle. More particularly it relates to a power supply for a space vehicle which offers a source of sustained thrust for the loss of a very small mass of fuel.

"Thus it would enable very high velocities to be attained in a space vehicle and in fact the prolonged acceleration of the vehicle may in some circumstances be used to simulate gravity."

The passengers would travel in a compartment a the top and would be protected from the radiation by a thick layer of metal above the reactor.

Eat your heart out, Richard Trevithick. Even Isambard Kingdom Brunel, when he built his great steamships SS *Great Britain* and *Great Western*, merely intended to extend the Great Western Railway beyond Bristol to New York.

Need I say that the British Rail flying saucer was never built. The patent expired in 1976 due to non-payment of renewal fees.

The public remained unaware of the existence of the plans until the story was broken by *The Guardian* on 31 May 1978, and over the ensuing years it resurfaced as a novelty item in the press from time to time.

The patent was 'rediscovered' in the archives in 2006, and a group of nuclear scientists examined the design. It was said to be not only expensive and very inefficient but wholly unworkable, which much of the technology it aimed to use, such as nuclear fusion, not having even been discovered. Michel van Baal of the European Space Agency in The Netherlands said: "I have had a look at the plans, and they don't look very serious to me at all."

He explained that the saucer would have needed an "unbelievable" amount of energy to fly. "I doubt whether, even if it was developed, it would ever be practical," he said.

Four decades on, exactly what British Rail was thinking of with its own 'flying train' remains unclear. Was there some kind of belief that just as steam technology quickly made huge advances in the wake of Stephenson's Rocket winning the Rainhill Trials and setting the blueprint for the path of locomotive development, so space technology travel might soon become the norm rather than the exception, and the patent application was therefore merely a means of 'marking out future territory'?

Indeed, much of what first appeared in science fiction has become part of everyday life.

The USS Enterprise in *Star Trek* has, it seems, far more in common with the laws of physics and predicted potential future technology than the British Rail 'space vehicle.' The makers of the series have hired teams of experts to ensure that storylines, no matter how far fetched, are at least theoretically possible.

Martin Cooper, the inventor of the world's first cellular phone, the Motorola Dyna-Tac, said he was inspired by watching Captain James T Kirk talking over his communicator device.

Early computers developed in the mid-20th century were massive machines taking up whole rooms, like the World War Two Colossus decoding machines at Bletchley Park used to crack Nazi ciphers. However, the Enterprise crew had hand-held computers that could be worn on a belt, known as tricorders. These inspired the inventors of the personal computer and the Palm Pilot, the first commercially-produced hand-held portable computers.

Also from the *Star Trek* stable came the concept of medical imaging technology, where patients could be diagnosed without painful exploratory surgery.

So one day British Rail may have the last laugh with its flying saucer, provided it manages to hone all the technology to perfection. As it stands, the doubting experts who examined the patent said that even if it could be made to work, and flew over the 'Flying Scotsman' route from King's Cross to Edinburgh Waverley, every field on either side of the track would be likely to be incinerated.

The Great Western Railway launched its own air service in 1933. Services flew between Plymouth, Cardiff and Castle Bromwich, using a three-engined Westland Wessex supplied by Imperial Airways, rather than interplanetary craft.

CHAPTER TWENTY NINE

BRITAIN'S SMALLEST PUBLIC RAILWAY

Norfolk Hero heads past the relocated Great Eastern Railway signalbox from Swainsthorpe, a station on the main London to Norwich line which closed in 1954.

FOR DECADES, THE Romney Hythe & Dymchurch Railway claimed to be the world's smallest public railway, the type of question that inevitably arises in pub quizzes. The claim was accurate, as the 13½-mile 15in gauge line which boasts a double track section on which to run its miniature versions of main line Pacific locomotives, has always offered a timetabled service. It answered the call of duty when, during World War Two, it ran armoured troop trains as part of Britain's sea defences, and in recent times has operated daily school services.

The 'world's smallest' title was seized by the 12¼in gauge Réseau Guerlédan in France in 1978. However, that line closed the following year and the title reverted back to Kent...for a few months.

Norfolk Hero in steam at Walsingham station.

The crown was then seized, permanently it seems, by a fresh Young Pretender, in the form of Norfolk's 10¼in gauge Wells and Walsingham Light Railway which opened that year.

The story of the railway dates back to 1972, with the building of *Edmund Hannay*, an 0-4-2T, by Norfolk engineer David King. Four years later, the locomotive's owner, retired Lieutenant Commander Roy Francis, opened the mile-long 10¼in gauge Wells Harbour Railway on a green field site at Wells-next-the-Sea. The line runs in a straight line from the town to a holiday camp near the sand dunes, past the home of Wells Town FC, and serving a true public transport purpose.

Roy sold the line in order to develop a longer 10¼in gauge line on the trackbed of the former Great Eastern Railway branch from Wymondham to Wells, which was opened on 1 December 1857 by the Norfolk Railway and closed to passengers in stages from 1964 to 1969 after the Beeching Axe fell. The southern part of the branch has been revived as the Mid-Norfolk Railway.

The Wells & Walsingham Light Railway is four miles long (making it the world's longest 10¼in gauge line) and links the outskirts of the town to Walsingham, a major pilgrimage centre since medieval times and famous for its shrines in honour of the Virgin Mary. The ruins of two medieval monastic houses are nearby. The terminus at Walsingham lies to the north of the original station.

The first major task in building the new light railway was the excavation of Barnard's Cutting, which had been infilled with 3,000 tons of refuse which had to be excavated to make way for tracklaying. Despite the excavation, the section was left with a 1-in-29 gradient which was not there under British Railways, and it was finally restored to the original 1-in-60 by engineers from the National Construction Training College who excavated another 17,000 tons of material in 1999.

Pilgrim, an 0-6-0 tank engine, also built by David King, launched the public service on 6 April 1982.

Five years later, a new locomotive arrived. It was *Norfolk Hero*, a superheated 2-6-2+2-6-2 Garratt locomotive, a British-designed articulated type which had always been better received in Third World countries than its own. Until the South African Railways NGG16 Garratts were reimported for use on the rebuilt Welsh Highland Railway, *Norfolk Hero*, which had been named after Admiral Lord Nelson, was the only Garratt operating in Britain.

A redundant signalbox was relocated from Swainsthorpe to Wells, and converted to form a shop and tearoom.

A second Garratt, red-liveried *Norfolk Heroine*, entered service in 2011. The name recalls Edith Cavell, the British nurse executed by the Germans in World War One.

The line has intermediate halts at Warham St Mary and Wighton, and two diesel locomotives.

Edmund Hannay, *which 'started' the Wells Harbour Railway, and which in 2010 was a prime exhibit in the Seaside Railways Exhibition at Cleethorpes.*

CHAPTER THIRTY
STEAM ENGINES THAT THOUGHT THEY WERE DIESELS

Vale of Rheidol Railway 2-6-2T No 9 Prince of Wales *in British Rail corporate blue livery in the mid-seventies.*

BRITISH RAIL INTRODUCED its corporate blue livery in 1964, and within a few years, every locomotive owned by the national operator carried it. Coaches were painted in matching blue and grey, and the uniform image stayed very much that way until the early eighties, when some variations became commonplace, and finally died a death only with the privatisation of the national network in the nineties.

BR Blue to enthusiasts is like Marmite: some loved it, and clamour to see preserved diesels carry it today: others hated it with a vengeance, being reminiscent of the 'one size fits all' era where so much of the steam era infrastructure was swept away in the name of progress and the railway of the seventies lacked the character of individuality.

British Rail steam haulage – on standard gauge – officially ended on 11 August 1968. when the 'Fifteen Guinea Special' carried enthusiasts from Liverpool Lime Street to Manchester Victoria and back. It was the last British Rail steam-hauled passenger train over the national network,

Immediately afterwards, all steam haulage on the British main line was banned, with one exceptional – LNER A3 Pacific No 4472 *Flying Scotsman*, which had previously-booked commitments.

Nonetheless, steam was still to be found on British Rail in two sectors. Firstly, the use of steam-powered self-propelled cranes for use in breakdown and maintenance trains lasted for another two decades.

Secondly, one British Rail line uniquely continued to carry passengers on trains hauled by steam locomotives inherited from the Great Western Railway.

This 'odd man out', the sole chink in the steam ban armour, was the 1ft 11¾in gauge Vale of Rheidol Railway which runs between Aberystwyth and Devil's Bridge in central Wales.

While British Rail's London Midland Region made this single exception as far as steam was concerned, no other ground was given.

For the three engines had all to be repainted from Brunswick green into BR corporate blue, with carriages adopting a livery to match.

The engines even carried the famous BR double-arrow logo, which also came in during

1964 and outlived the nationalised company by being adopted as a definitive logo to mark stations on the national network and road signs pointing to them even today.

The 11¾-mile line which had opened on 22 December 1902 survived because someone in the London Midland hierarchy saw the success of the enthusiast-led preservation schemes that had successfully taken over other Welsh lines like the Talyllyn, Ffestiniog and Welshpool & Llanfair railways as tourist attractions, and realised that the Vale of Rheidol could do the same.

The line, built by an independent company, was formally taken over by the Cambrian Railways in 1913, and the latter became part of the GWR empire at the Grouping of 1922, with significant investment.

Three new locomotives were built at Swindon in 1923: the new No 7 and No 8 were followed in 1924 by a 'refurbished' No 2 *Prince of Wales*, which was in effect a new locomotive built from a third set of parts, described as a 'heavy overhaul', just to satisfy the GWR accountants, whereas the original No 2 had been scrapped. Nos 7 and 8 were named *Owain Glyndwr* and *Llywelyn* respectively in 1926. None of the original locomotives survived.

The GWR also built new passenger coaches to cater for the summer tourist traffic, eliminating the previous practice of carrying extra peak period passengers in freight wagons.

At nationalisation on 1 January 1948, the line became part of the Western Region, and despite rumours of closure in the mid-fifties, it was transferred to the London Midland Region in 1963.

Following the highly unusual and eyebrow-raising decision by British Rail to retain the line running, despite the mass wave of closures of rural branch lines demanded by Dr Richard Beeching throughout the rest of the country, the Rail Blue livery and double arrow logo were applied to the locomotives and carriages in 1967.

Under the TOPS numbering arrangements for diesel and electric locomotives that was introduced by British Rail, the trio were designated Class 98 and were nominally numbered 98007–98009, but they never carried these numbers.

The London Midland Region soon regretted the decision to keep the line open. Partially because it was still run by paid staff rather than volunteers as on other Welsh narrow gauge lines, losses mounted, and in 1967 British Rail made plans to close it. However, the little railway was reprieved largely thanks to Transport Minister Barbara Castle, who visited it on 1 July that year.

In the eighties, the Rail Blue livery gave way to more traditional liveries that the locomotives and stock carried in the past, and afterwards British Rail's last steam line looked like any other heritage railway of the period.

Under British Rail, track maintenance suffered somewhat. On 26 May 1986, trackwork

Carrying Rail Blue, No 8 Llywelyn is seen at Pont yr Fynach in July 1984.

Today's livery: No 8 Llywellyn proudly wears its Great Western Railway maker's colours. The carriages are painted in matching chocolate and cream. Rail Blue is unlikely ever to return!

came apart at a curve near the 6½ mile post.

A question was subsequently tabled in the House of Commons asking why British Rail was wasting its time on running a steam tourist line.

Two years later, British Rail decided to sell the line. In April 1989 it was bought by Tony Hills and Peter Rampton, owners of the Brecon Mountain Railway, a tourist line near Merthyr Tydfil.

The line was one of only two pieces of the operational national rail network to be sold to a private owner without interruption of regular passenger services. The first was South Devon's Paignton to Kingswear line, another former GWR branch which in 1972 was sold directly to

Dart Valley Railway plc, which tried to carry on running the same services as under British Rail until economics dictated seasonal running only. It is now known as the Dartmouth Steam Railway & Riverboat Company.

In 1991, the Brecon partnership split, with Tony Hills keeping the Brecon line and Peter Rampton taking the Vale of Rheidol Railway. Eventually, the Vale of Rheidol Railway was transferred to the Phyllis Rampton Narrow Gauge Railway Trust, which is the line's major shareholder.

In 2000, the Railway Heritage Committee, a statutory body which has the powers to 'claim' main line artefacts including rolling stock for preservation, designated the Vale of Rheidol Railway's three steam locomotives, 16 GWR bogie carriages, 11 four-wheel wagons and a guard's van. Under the designation, the items cannot be sold or scrapped without permission of the committee, the powers of which encompass any organisation which was once a subsidiary of British Rail.

Despite its privatisation, the Vale of Rheidol Railway still has the company registration number that was established by British Rail.

GWR livery for locomotives and rolling stock is the norm today, and current disdain for the line's BR Blue era is so great that it has to be mentioned in hushed tones amongst supporters, or not at all.

Bizarre road bridge: the Devil's Bridge, a prime attraction for tourists arriving by train at the station of the same name, is a series of three bridges built on top of each other over nine centuries, crossing the gorge of the Afon Mynach below. The poet William Wordsworth wrote about the "torrent at the Devil's Bridge", the Mynach waterfalls below being a major tourist magnet since the 18th century and a prime source of passenger revenue on the railway, helping to keep it open into the BR Blue era when all other steam on the national railway died out.

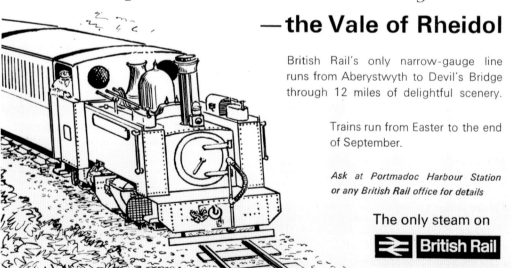

Another of the Great Little Trains of Wales
—the Vale of Rheidol

British Rail's only narrow-gauge line runs from Aberystwyth to Devil's Bridge through 12 miles of delightful scenery.

Trains run from Easter to the end of September.

Ask at Portmadoc Harbour Station or any British Rail office for details

The only steam on
British Rail

A 1970s British Rail advertisement for its only steam line.

CHAPTER THIRTY ONE
STEAM ON ONE RAIL

The restored Patiala State Monorail Tramway steam monorail locomotive in action at the Indian Railway Museum.

TO TAKE THE WORD 'railway' literally, there should be one rail, not two. And who not use just one rail?

As with the steam-powered railway locomotive, Britain can claim a world first in the field of passenger-carrying monorails.

In 1825, the horse-worked Cheshunt Railway, designed by Henry Robinson Palmer to carry bricks from a quarry to the River Lea, carried passengers at its opening. It was also the first railway line to be opened in Hertfordshire.

The world's first monorail is said to have been created in Russia in 1820 by inventor Ivan Elmanov in Myachkovo village near Moscow, but the wheels were set on the track itself, not on the carriages, which were horse drawn. It was Palmer who in 1821 took out the first patent, and built a monorail at Deptford Dockyard in London.

It took more than half a century for steam to replace horses on one rail as they had done on two. In 1876, General Le-Roy Stone demonstrated the first steam-driven monorail at the United States Centennial Exposition in Philadelphia in 1876. It comprised a double-decker vehicle with two main wheels, the rear one driven by a rotary steam engine.

A modified version of this monorail was used to transport oil drilling equipment and personnel over a four-mile line between Bradford and Gilmore in Pennsylvania. However, local residents also began using it after intermediate stations were added

The worst disaster in monorail history took place on this line on 27 January 1879 when a new and more powerful engine coupled to a flat car full of officials was run at high speed to show what it was capable of doing. The boiler exploded and the train crashed into a creek, killing the driver, fireman and three passengers, leaving the rest severely injured. The monorail was abandoned soon afterwards.

In 1907, the first section of a monorail, the Patiala State Monorail Tramway, opened over the six miles between Bassi and Sirhind (6 miles) in the Punjab by a Colonel Bowles, the state engineer. It expanded to 50 miles with lines linking Sirhind to Alampura, and Patiala with Bhavanigarh.

The track was a single rail running on the roadside, the trains kept upright by a single outrigger wheel which ran on the road, similar to a stabiliser on a child's bicycle.

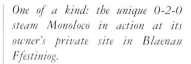

One of a kind: the unique 0-2-0 steam Monoloco in action at its owner's private site in Blaenau Ffestiniog.

At first mules hauled the trains, but between 1907-9, the German firm of Orenstein & Koppel supplied four 0-3-0 steam locomotives with double flanged driving wheels.

Maintenance difficulties and competition from more efficient and less complex transport led to the demise of the monorail in October 1927.

In 1962, the monorail stock was accidentally discovered by English enthusiast Mike Satow

Rich Morris' Monocolo in action at his private monorail near Blaenau Ffestiniog, a town far better known for the Ffestiniog Railway and its double Fairlies, as seen in Chapter 5.

half buried in the former permanent way department's scrapyard. One of the engines, No 4, which dates from 1909, was retrieved and restored to working order by the Northern Railway's Amritsar workshops. The line's chief engineer's private inspection car was also found and restored.

A length of monorail was later laid at the Indian Railway Museum in New Delhi so that the pair could operate there.

On Sunday 13 December 1997, a modern-day steam 'Monoloco' made its maiden run over a short length of track at Sunbury-on-Thames in Middlesex.

From the chassis upwards it looked every bit a typical industrial narrow gauge tank engine resplendent in its bright blue livery.

However, the wheels gave the game away: it had just two, and is believed to be the world's only 0-2-0 tank engine.

Its appearance was the culmination of a 25-year dream by enthusiast Rich Morris, who previously owned the Gloddfa Ganol narrow gauge railway and mining centre at Blaenau Ffestiniog, which closed in 1997.

The Monoloco was built by engineering company Century Millwrights on Platts Eyot, a small island in the River Thames, over two years.

Rich, who had been collecting mono rail equipment for 30 years, had drawn up rough sketches of his dream project and given them to project engineer John Vineer, who made a number of refinements to create the blueprint of a locomotive that would work.

Standing 6ft high and 11ft long, the locomotive was built on the chassis of a Metalair Ltd wagon previously used on an industrial monorail line. In 1983, Rich had acquired the manufacturing rights of Metalair Ltd of Wokingham, Britain's only commercial monorail builder.

His locomotive runs on driving wheels with double flanges which straddle a triangular section running rail an inch wide at the top of the rail. Outriding stabiliser wheels at the front and back riding on the 3in bottom section of the rail keep the Monoloco steady.

The height of the track can be altered from 14in above ground level, to a maximum 7ft 8in, using stands of different sizes. That system was developed in the 1940s by Road Machines (Drayton) Ltd. of Middlesex, which produced internal combustion and diesel-powered monorail equipment for temporary use on building sites.

The Monoloco made its public debut at the International Model Railway Exhibition at Kensington Olympia in December 1997.

It now runs on a system developed by Rich at a private site in Blaenau Ffestiniog, where open days are very occasionally held.

CHAPTER THIRTY TWO

A GARDEN RAILWAY *BIGGER* THAN THE 'REAL ONE'!

HAVING YOUR OWN garden railway is a lifelong dream of many enthusiasts. Normally such lines fall very much into the model category, O gauge, Gauge 1 or G scale, sizes that would be too cramped in the average house.

There are those lucky enough to have a bigger outfit – maybe a miniature railway, using a 5in or 7¼in gauge locomotive and stock to take people on rides round the back garden.

The idea of building a scaled-down version of the 'big' railway for pleasure purposes dates back to Sir Arthur Heywood's Duffield Bank Railway in Derbyshire, which opened in 1874.

He explored the possibility of using scaled-down versions of 'normal' railways, some running on tracks as narrow as 15in, for mining, quarrying, agriculture and other industries.

Despite trying to market the idea commercially, he had only one taker, the Duke of Westminster, who commissioned him to build a 4½-mile 15in gauge network linking his

Finnish Hr1 class 4-6-2 No 1016 Lady Patricia has been bought to steam in Berkshire. Peckett saddle tank Hornpipe passes by on the standard gauge line alongside the 5ft broad gauge track.

A young David Buck on the footplate of then brand-new Britannia Pacific No 70035 Rudyard Kipling *at Ipswich in 1953. Then, it was almost every schoolboy's dream to be a steam engine driver: David has now achieved it big time.*

David Buck in 2009, in the cab of his own Finnish Pacific in his back garden.

home at Eaton Hall in Cheshire to the Great Western Railway station sidings at Balderton on the Shrewsbury to Chester line.

It gripped the imagination and the concept took off, manifesting itself in seaside miniature railways, of which most traditional resorts had at least one during the 20th century, and bigger concerns like the Ravenglass & Eskdale or Romney, Hythe & Dymchurch Railways, which used locomotives based on reduced scale versions of main line types.

Yet what about the ultimate garden railway – one that is full size?

Narrow gauge is an obvious choice here. Chiltern Railways chairman Adrian Shooter has a 2ft gauge line, the Beeches Light Railway, with a former Darjeeling Himalayan Railway Sharp Stewart B class 0-4-0 saddle hauling a pair of replica coaches of the legendary Indian line which were built to order in the Ffestiniog Railway workshops at Boston Lodge.

The best known narrow gauge garden line was the late Reverend Teddy Boston's Cadeby Light Railway at his rectory in the Leicestershire village of the same name, which had a short 2ft gauge line in the garden. His collection was sold off by his widow in recent years and the line, opened to the public once a month from the mid-sixties onwards at a time when steam was disappearing fast from the national network, sadly is no more.

Today, there are several private locations where enthusiasts have bought old stations, renovated them and relaid standard gauge track, maybe to site an old carriage as a summerhouse, or even to bring in a small shunting locomotive. In some cases, standard gauge has been laid on a green field site: Peter Clark's Fulstow Railway near Louth in Lincolnshire, a stone's throw from the Lincolnshire Wolds Railway is one example, and is very rarely open to the public. The most extensive private system of this type is multi-millionaire enthusiast Sir William McAlpine's Fawley Hill Railway at his mansion home near Henley-on-Thames, which in 2010 marked its half centenary. Private steaming days have seen visiting locomotives brought in and rides in grounds where wallabies roam freely.

However, there is an enthusiast who has gone one better – and laid a broad gauge railway in his back garden – one that is built to both a wider track and loading gauge than used on the British national network!

David Buck, like his father Peter before him an enthusiast, became a hugely-successful businessman as managing director of a company which processes movie film for the likes of 20th Century Fox and in 1981 bought a half-timbered house which had previously been home to the late eccentric hairdresser 'Teasie Weasie' Raymond in a village near Windsor, with 12 acres of flat land at the back…and began building a 3½in gauge line.

Gripped by the railway-building bug, after a few years he set his sights on a standard gauge railway. Lengths of track were salvaged from various parts of Britain, including five points from the GWR Swindon Works which closed in 1986.

His first standard gauge locomotive was *Hornpipe*, Peckett 0-4-0 saddle tank No 1756 of

1928, which had spent its entire working life at a chalk quarry near Holborough in Kent owned by a cement manufacturer. It arrived at the Buckinghamshire Railway Centre from a scrapyard in 1972 and was restored to haul passenger trains, being sold on to David in 1985.

Hornpipe was followed by Hawthorn Leslie 0-6-0ST No 3138 of 1916, a former Corby steelworks engine, a long-term restoration project, and a 1942-built GWR 'Toad' brake van, which formed the first passenger carriage on David's line.

He also acquired ex-Buckinghamshire Railway Centre Aveling & Porter flywheel-driven four-wheeler No 8800 of 1917 *Sir Vincent*, which had seen industrial service in Erith in Kent.

However, in 2007, David went one better, and bought a 5ft gauge Finnish 4-6-2 – one that is both taller and wider than British Pacifics including *Flying Scotsman* and *Mallard*.

The locomotive was acquired from British businessman Nigel Sill, who runs heritage steam excursions in Finland. In the eighties, Nigel imported several Finnish steam

Lady Patricia, *awaiting restoration including a full retube.*

Traction engine-type Aveling & Porter steam locomotive Sir Vincent *in action on David's standard gauge line.*

locomotives to Britain for a Wild West theme park in Cornwall whose plans to build a railway never took off, and the locomotives were left to be stored in various places around Essex and North London.

The one David bought, Hr1 class No 1016, had been displayed at Enfield for several years. Built in 1955, it was one of a class off 22 built in Finland by Tampella and Lokomo between 1937-57. They were the biggest passenger locomotives built or used in Finland and remained the main locomotives used in the south of that country on express trains until 1963, when Hr12 class diesels took over. Along with the German Class 10s, the Hr1s were the last new built Pacifics built in Europe before the end of the steam era.

After dieselisation, several Finnish steam engines were stored at the Lievestuore military depot near Haapamäki to be used during times of crisis, when diesel oil would be hard to come by. The engines were packaged and protected against rusting and weather, until the eighties when it was finally decided that they would not be needed again.

David laid a 300-yard running line on which the locomotive, now named *Lady Patricia*, will eventually move up and down, while beginning the early stages of its restoration. The massive tender will have a wooden deck fitted at the rear, above the coal container, and seats will be fitted so passengers will be able to ride on it.

David has installed floodlighting so that the locomotive is illuminated at night and he can enjoy the sight of it from his bedroom window.

Unlike other preserved steam locomotives, it will never be hired to other railways, because nobody else in Britain has a 5ft gauge running line.

The line is never opened to the general public, but has hosted visits from groups like the Industrial Railway Society.

"One of the reasons why I bought the house before the property prices went up in the 1980s was that it had so much flat land a garden railway could be built," said David.

"The 5in gauge line was so much fun that I considered a full-size line and thought – why not? We had the space.

"You could not buy a British standard gauge Pacific, but I will soon have an even bigger 4-6-2 of my own running."

A behemoth in the woods awaits its turn to steam again.

CHAPTER THIRTY THREE

A BRANCH LINE RELAID –
FOR ONE DAY ONLY!

RAILWAYS PRESENT a conundrum. We earlier looked at Brunel's 7ft 0¼in broad gauge, and there are far wider tracks at industrial installations such as dockyards for rail-mounted cranes and power stations for movement of machinery.

In 2007, a Japanese firm called KK-Eishindo began producing the world's smallest commercially-produced electric model railway equipment with the rails just 3mm apart, under the banner of T gauge.

Most railway modellers in Britain today opt for OO gauge, 4mm to 1ft, with rails 16.5mm apart, or N gauge, 2mm to 1ft, rails 9mm apart. Those with large spaces and preferably back gardens can opt for O gauge, 7mm to 1ft, or G scale, where the rails are 45mm apart, and the scale depends on whatever country's stock is represented.

Above that, there are 3½in, 5in, 7¼in and 10¼in gauges, as 'models' get bigger and give way to the 'miniature railways' concept: at some point on this ascending scale, trains can begin physically carrying passengers. Beyond there, we have 15in, 18in and 2ft gauge, which may well be the true narrow gauge of 'full size' railways.

Models are a form of art, and one purpose of art is to represent reality. Therefore, in terms of size, where is the dividing line between a railway and a model?

Many would say when a railway runs a train capable of having passengers or freight, or when it operates a regular service.

This philosophical question was certainly tested in late August 2009 when a complete railway line was relaid, following years of campaigning by revivalists and local residents, not to 4ft 8½in gauge as they hoped, but to the very much smaller OO gauge!

In 1982, the final trains ran over the London & South Western railway's Barnstaple to Bideford, Torrington, Marland and Meeth line, which had remained open for freight in the form of ball clay traffic since the 'Beeching Axe' had fallen on passenger services in 1965.

Enthusiasts tried to save it from being ripped up, but Devon County Council acquired the trackbed from British Rail in the late eighties and turned it into a long-distance footpath and cycleway, now known as the Tarka Trail after Henry Williamson's legendary fictional otter who roamed these parts.

TV presenter James May and his new Barnstaple station, as seen on his Toy Stories *DVD released in 2009.*

Interchange: the new Bideford branch leaves Network Rail's Barnstaple station platform, terminus of the Tarka Line from Exeter.

Eventually, the revivalsits acquired the use of Bideford station, set up a static museum, laid some track, and in the early 21st century, ran some diesel shunter-hauled passenger rides over 400 yards of track. At Torrington station, which had been converted into the Puffing Billy pub and restaurant, owner Phil Simkin, began a heritage railway scheme of his own, planning to relay as much standard gauge track as possible along part of the Tarka Trail from his establishment northwards

There were those who never stopped campaigning for the old railway to be relaid to provide passenger services to Barnstaple and on to Exeter via the Tarka Line.

Their wish came true on 24 August 2009. when once again, Bulleid West Country light Pacific No 34045 *Ottery St Mary* chugged its way from Barnstaple to Bideford hauling a rake of three Pullman cars forming a modern-day 'Atlantic Coast Express', cheered on by thousands of well wishers.

It was nothing less than an attempt to build the world's longest-ever model railway, to feature in television presenter James May's BBC2 *Toy Stories* series, with an episode screened at the end of the year.

Close-up view of the 'reborn' Barnstaple station.

The loneliest model railway in the world running along an empty section of the Tarka trail.

Modelmaker Hornby provided 10 miles of OO gauge track to lay on the Tarka Trail, and the trains to go with it. As a mile in OO scale is represented by 69.29ft of track, the total length in model terms was a whopping 762 miles. For comparison purposes, the length of Britain's railway network in 2010 was 10,106 miles, and the distance from Land's End to John O'Groats in 874 miles.

At around £2 per yard, it was estimated that the track would have cost £35,000 to buy from a model shop.

An army of 400 helpers including around 60 different community groups including scouts laid the track on the Tarka Trail and installed 12-volt batteries at intervals to maintain the current. Where the track passed houses, the opportunity to boost the voltage using mains electricity was taken. Separate teams were delegated to operate isolated sections in a bid to ensure that twigs, stones or other objects did not mysteriously appear on the line.

Among the other feats in the *Toy Stories* series also filmed in August 2009 were a Scalextric recreation of the Brooklands motor racing circuit on the original site near Weybridge, Surrey, and the building of a full-size house built out of Lego bricks in the middle of the Denbies Wine Estate in Dorking, Surrey.

The Hornby Hitachi Javelin train whizzes to success.

The full size railway as it was: no 2p coin could short-circuit this one! Ivatt 2-6-2T No 41314 pulls into Instow on 8 September 1961.

James said that he picked the Tarka Trail for the world record attempt not only because people wanted to see the old line rebuilt, but because of the beautiful scenery.

Five traction units were also supplied by Hornby for the attempt to run the full length of the new line.

The first trains set off from a specially-created new Barnstaple station, a few feet from the canopy of the Network Rail version and its buffer stops, in the early afternoon.

Some of the Hornby locomotives managed to reach a real speed of more than 1mph.

Sadly, none of them reached Bideford, due to what Hornby marketing manager Simon Kohler described as "silliness."

At one point along the line, 2p coins laid on the line caused a short circuit and blew a battery. Elsewhere, lengths of track were stolen as dusk fell.

When the last locomotive still running finally rolled into Instow – where the original full-size signalbox has been preserved - at 12.30am the next day, everyone decided to call a halt to the proceedings.

Simon Kohler stoutly refused to concede defeat. "Even though the last locomotive gave up the ghost at Instow, we did link the track," he said.

"We refused to let the spoilsports ruin things. It was a really brave effort and the strength

An example of the Hornby Javelin train which ran from Barnstaple to Instow.

One of the tracklaying gangs makes progress.

The track was looped at several intervals to ensure that the world record would be attained even if anything went wrong with far-flung parts of the instant railway, fears that turned out to be justified.

and tenacity of the helpers was simply extraordinary.

James May said that despite the vandalism, the stunt had been a success: "I was amazed and touched by the amount of people who turned up on the day just to see my toy train go past."

The contest was not 'won' by the Bulleid Pacific, typical of traction over the LSWR 'Withered Arm', of which the route was part. Instead, honours went to Hornby's model of the new Hitachi Class 395 electric multiple units, the only train that set out from Bideford that managed to reach as far as Instow.

The feat clearly switched many people on to the potential that a revived railway could offer the region.

Within three weeks of the stunt, Torridge councillor Miranda Cox publicly called for the old line to be restored, but at a scale where 1ft really means 1ft. "The engineering is always there to build new roads, so why not a railway? It would be great for tourism, ease congestion and reduce emissions," she said.

May repeated his TV stunt of building the world's longest model railway when the line was relaid for a head-to-head race against a team of German enthusiasts on Saturday 16 April 2011. Crowds turned out to see May and wine expert Oz Clarke win – with a 1972 Hornby model of *Flying Scotsman*, the world's fastest steam locomotive.

End of the line…for now? Track has been relaid at Torrington station, now the Puffing Billy pub and restaurant, and the owner hopes to extend it as a heritage railway northwards towards Bideford, but as a full-size railway, unlike James May's escapade.

CHAPTER THIRTY FOUR
MAN'S MIX AND MATCH MISFITS

THE ISLE OF MAN is a Mecca for transport enthusiasts. Three vintage railways dating from Victorian times still form part of the island's public transport network today.

The 15½-mile 3ft gauge Isle of Man Railway from Douglas to Port Erin is the sole surviving part of a once far more extensive steam network that also ran from Douglas to Peel and Ramsey, and which dates from 1874. Then there is the 17½-mile 3ft gauge overhead pick-up Manx Electric Railway which runs along the coast from Douglas to Ramsey, via Laxey, from where the 3ft 6in gauge Snaefell Mountain Railway winds 4½ miles to the summit of the island's highest peak.

Not to mention of course, the Douglas Horse Tramway, the 2ft gauge Groudle Glen Railway and the 19in gauge Great Laxey Mine Railway.

All of these are markedly different from each other, beginning with separate gauges and/or modes of traction.

Yet what would happen if…you tried to force square pegs into round holes, and exchanged motive power and rolling stock between the main three lines?

Surely if would be like a team of cricketers turning up at the wrong destination and being asked to play football? Yet it has happened, and in 2010, the Isle of Man Post Office issued a special series of stamps to highlight bizarre exchanges on the island's lines.

With the centenary of the Manx Electric Railway in 1993 and that of the Snaefell Mountain Railway in 1995, Isle of Man Railways staged some weird some unique celebratory events.

Steam locomotives had been used to build both lines. Indeed, an extra 3ft gauge rail had been laid on the Snaefell line to allow Dubs 0-6-0 tank engine No 15 *Caledonia*, built in 1885 originally for the Manx Northern Railway, to haul construction trains to the top.

Beyer Peacock 2-4-0T No 2 *Derby* had been used to build the section of the Manx Electric between Laxey and Ramsey.

As it had been scrapped in 1951, as part of the 1993 Year of the Railways celebrations, it was decided to use sister No 4 *Loch* hauling closed trailers Nos 57 and 58 between Laxey and the Dhoon, including a sustained gradient of two miles far steeper than any on the steam line.

For the Snaefell centenary, It was decided to temporarily relay that third rail from

Bungalow Halt to the Summit to repeat *Caledonia's* feat. The locomotive was taken out of the Port Erin railway museum and restored to full working order in time for the centenary celebrations, dubbed the International Railway Festival. *Caledonia* was repainted into Manx Northern Railway colours and successfully hauled a trailer to the mountain top.

Steam 125 in 1998 marked 125 years of the steam railway's existence, with Beyer Peacock 2-4-0T No 1 *Sutherland* also taken out of the museum and restored to full working order. It too was steamed on the Manx Electric Railway, in a southerly direction from Laxey to Fairy Cottage.

Even more bizarrely, an electric car from the Manx Electric Railway ran on the steam line between Douglas and Port Erin, with Car No 33 powered by a diesel generator concealed in a luggage van.

These feats of bending island railway reality may never be repeated, but the stamps tell the story.

The 35p stamp shows *Caledonia* approaching Snaefull summit with trailer No 57, while the 36p stamp depicts *Sutherland* alongside Manx Electric Railway Car No 1 in Laxey station for the Steam 125 celebrations. One of the oldest working steam locomotives in the world was photographed alongside the oldest working tramcar in the world.

The 55p stamp shows *Caledonia* passing the rock face at Bulgham, the highest point of the coastal tramway, with Manx Electric Railway closed trailer No 58.

The 88p value stamp depicts *Loch* approaching Skinscoe curve on the Manx Electric Railway with trailers Nos 57 and 58.

The £1.32 stamp has Manx Electric Car No 33 approaching the top of the climb out of Douglas to Keristal summit on the steam line.

The £1.46 stamp shows a double headed special featuring *Loch* and sister No 11 *Maitland* double heading on the steam line, but with *Loch* unusually travelling bunker first.

Might we one day see *Flying Scotsman* run on the Blackpool Tramway, or a London Underground tube train take the East Coast Main Line to York, I mischievously wonder?